HERE COMES THE SUN

Here Comes The Sun

MOMENTS WITH GOD IN THE SEASONS OF CANCER

JOELLEN PUTNAM

HEART NOTES

PRESS

Dedication

This book is written in memory of Christine A. McCormack (July 17, 1962 – October 17, 2007).

It is dedicated to my amazing husband, Marty, and to my unshakeable friend Nadine Brennan. You two held me up and carried my weight and tears on your shoulders. You were there for me every moment, loving me, listening to me, encouraging me, making me laugh, holding me close, protecting me, praying relentlessly for me, and speaking life and hope into every part of my being. Because of your love and your strength, our cord of three strands could not be broken. *Thank you* will never be enough.

And to my children, Danielle and Zack, who I adore and love more than anything on earth. I hope you can see the arms of Jesus wrapped around you in every one of my stories, and that you will understand how my fierce love for you inspired me to kick cancer's butt.

Contents

INTRODUCTION

Dedication 5

My Story 9

Your Story 15

WINTER ~ DIAGNOSIS

1: The First Chapter 21

2: His Compassion 25

3: The First Night................................. 29

4: Childlike Faith 33

5: Today 39

6: "Jesus" 45

7: Trauma 49

8: The Prayer of Relinquishment 53

SPRING ~ TREATMENT

9: Partnership with God 61

10: Decisions....................................... 65

11: Good Things 71

12: Guarding Your Heart...................... 75

13: Grace... 79

14: Resting in His Shadow 85

15: The Power of Prayer....................... 91

16: A Trip to the Wilderness................. 95

17: The Heart of the Matter 101

SUMMER ~ RECOVERY

18: Heart Scars 111
19: The Temptation of Fear 115
20: The Question of Recurrence 121
21: Encouraging Words 127
22: My Trophy 131
23: His Presence 135
24: Mary 143

AUTUMN ~ TRANSFORMATION

25: The Depth of God's Love.......................... 149
26: A Day of Salvation............................. 155
27: Forty 159
28: A Kingdom Assignment 165
29: Imperfect Faith......................... 171
30: Kingdom Destiny...................... 175
31: More than Ribbons 185

Appendix I 191
Appendix II...................................... 199
Appendix III..................................... 207
Appendix IV..................................... 217

Afterword.. 221
Acknowledgements................................ 223
Author Bio 226
End Notes 227
Index of Ways God Speaks to Us 229
Heart Notes...................................... 231

My Story

Give praise to the LORD, proclaim his name;
make known among the nations what he has done.
Sing to him, sing praise to him; tell of all his wonderful acts.
Glory in his holy name;
let the hearts of those who seek the LORD rejoice.
Look to the LORD and his strength;
seek his face always.

Psalm 105:1–4

I was a thirty-nine-year-old wife and stay-at-home mom with two young children when I was diagnosed with Stage 1b invasive breast cancer. I was stunned. *How did this happen? Am I going to die? What will happen to my children if I'm gone? How long has death been lurking in my body?* The questions were endless and terrifying, but one thing was certain: I knew Jesus. With my Savior by my side, I knew I could get through anything, even two surgeries, three and a half months of chemotherapy, ten years of hormonal treatment, and many months of depression.

Like the seasons in the natural world, the seasons of

cancer have distinct characteristics—some dark, some beautiful, some bittersweet, and each with a transition from one to the next. The shock of the diagnosis is like a brutal winter suspending life beneath its frozen terrain. The transition to treatment is like the passage to spring, a season of hope and new life. Summer is like recovery, a period of rest and rejuvenation. And we observe the changing colors of autumn in reflection of how we, too, have changed.

As I confronted the ugly disease that invaded my life, God revealed Himself to me through little encounters. In *My Utmost for His Highest*, Oswald Chambers notes, "The things that make God dear to us are not so much His great big blessings as the tiny things, because they reveal His amazing intimacy with us."[1] This book is the story of my intimate encounters with God as He carried me through the seasons of cancer. Like a sheep who knows her shepherd's call, I followed my Savior's voice (see John 10:1–16; 16:13).

The voice of the Lord is a gentle whisper in our hearts, a "sense" or "inner voice" that travels through the Holy Spirit. It's easy to dismiss the Lord's voice as our own thoughts, but the Bible testifies that indeed God speaks to us, and His children recognize His voice (see John 10:27). Hearing God is a key theme in this book, so you'll see highlights along the way. I've noted thirty different ways the Lord spoke to me.

During cancer, my focus was completely on physical healing. I wanted to survive so I could be the mom my children needed. But the healing God wanted for me was much deeper than physical; inside me was an emotional cancer growing deeper than the tumor in my flesh. Jesus touched every part of me and because of Him, today I am free.

Cancer is a difficult road to travel. It's painful to endure, impossible to understand. There are times when our tears overwhelm us, when we're tempted to give up. But through it all, there are times when we encounter Jesus. Those are the times to keep.

God speaks
through intimate encounters.

TO EVERYTHING
THERE IS A SEASON

Ecclesiastes 3:1–8

There is a time for everything,
and a season for every activity under the heavens:
a time to be born and a time to die,
a time to plant and a time to uproot,
a time to kill and a time to heal,
a time to tear down and a time to build,
a time to weep and a time to laugh,
a time to mourn and a time to dance,
a time to scatter stones and a time to gather them,
a time to embrace and a time to refrain from embracing,
a time to search and a time to give up,
a time to keep and a time to throw away,
a time to tear and a time to mend,
a time to be silent and a time to speak,
a time to love and a time to hate,
a time for war and a time for peace.

Your Story

To everything there is a season,
a time to every purpose under heaven.

Ecclesiastes 3:1 NKJV

*H*ere Comes the Sun tells my story, but its purpose is to nurture *your* story as you navigate the seasons of cancer. Just as the Holy Spirit awakened my spiritual senses to see the Lord's face and hear His voice, He will do the same for you. Not in a way that's formulaic, but in a way that's unique to your relationship with Him, whatever that may be. Writing my story was a transformative process, and I encourage you to write yours too. There is healing in the process, and healing when we look back and remember. Often, when we reflect on our experiences, we see God where we didn't see Him before. There is joy where there used to be only sorrow.

The power of remembrance is a major theme in the Old Testament. At significant points in their journey, the Israelites built altars of stone to remember what God did for them (1 Samuel 7:12; Genesis 28:16–20;

Exodus 17:15; Judges 6:24). These stones had power because a story was written inside them—but that power could only be released when the story was told or remembered. When the children of Israel faced trouble, they forgot their stories about God and what He did for them. Tragically, they abandoned their faith and reverted to old patterns of thinking and behavior. The consequences were disastrous for them. The same is true for us.

We are naturally prone to forget our blessings if we're not intentional about preserving them. When we look back on what God did for us in the past, it gives us faith that He will do it again. Our stories are a powerful weapon against the "What if..." lies of Satan. I don't always have energy to defend myself against those lies, but I always have my stories. They encourage me, empower me, and inspire me every time I read them. Our stories encourage other people too.

The "Moments with God" section at the end of each chapter will help you engage with the Lord and create your own stone of remembrance. Use it to process your thoughts, questions, and emotions, and keep them in a journal. You don't have to be a good writer, just an honest one. If journaling is not your thing and you'd rather keep it simple, there's a "Heart Notes" section at the end of the book to jot meaningful words and nuggets. Even if you don't pen your stories on paper, you can write them on the tablet of your heart. The important thing is to keep them safe.

If you're an artist, draw a picture as you meet with the Lord. Craft a poem or a song, choreograph a dance, or simply talk with Him. Take a walk in the forest or along the river and look for Him in His creation. Listen to worship songs, play an instrument you enjoy, or meditate. There is healing in silence. The Lord reveals Himself in myriad ways so look for Him, think about Him, and engage with Him daily. Be mindful of His ever-presence.

Friend, God did not give you cancer, He gave you a Savior. No matter your diagnosis or prognosis, the Lord will be with you every moment. And one day, when you look back on your story, you won't remember the tears; your heart will remind you that nearness to Jesus is everything you need.

God speaks
through our memories.

HELD BY GRACE

You may pray
for me to help you
write your story
but don't you see?
First you must agree
to let yourself be
held by Me

by Jai Gaurangi

Winter

WINTER MEDITATION

There's something to be said for
the way the threads of months gone by
are gently braided together by
winter's nimble, frosty fingers.
For however frayed they may appear,
every strand of joy, pain, hope, loss,
happiness and despair are uniquely ours,
filaments of love woven into
the tapestry of life,
an intricate masterpiece sewn
as we gently navigate
our way back home.

by Jai Gaurangi

1

The First Chapter

Many are the plans in a person's heart,
but it is the LORD's purpose that prevails.

Proverbs 19:21

Have you ever met someone or visited a new place that instantly felt like home? It happened to my family in the fall of 2006 when we visited our friend's church. We had no intention of staying long-term, but we were so captivated by the presence of the Holy Spirit, we decided to make it our new church home. A few Sundays after our "visit," we ran into a couple we knew from my husband's workplace. It was one of those strange experiences where you recognize someone out of context and feel a little woozy and confused. We had connected with this couple briefly at social functions, but when we saw each other that day at church and realized we had a common faith, we quickly became good friends.

Several months later, my friend shared with me the heartbreaking story of her lifelong girlfriend, Christine, who was experiencing her third recurrence of breast cancer. It was Stage 4 and Christine wasn't doing well. Whenever we got together, we prayed for Christine, and I did my best to support my friend as she supported hers.

I often thought about Christine and her young daughter. I couldn't imagine what it must be like for a mother to know she was dying. Christine had no family history of breast cancer, nor did she have any risk factors. She had been a healthy, vibrant, active thirty-eight-year-old mom when she was first ambushed by cancer.

I was thinking about our commonalities one morning when I realized I hadn't done a breast exam in a long time. So I did one right then and was very surprised to find a lump. I was even more surprised three weeks later when I, too, was diagnosed with invasive breast cancer. I was among the 5 percent of women under the age of forty who are diagnosed each year.

God speaks
through the lives of other people.

Moments with God

Learning that you have cancer is a traumatic experience. If it's too painful for you to recall the details of your diagnosis, skip this section for now. Then, when you are ready, come back to it, because the Lord wants to heal you of this trauma.

1. Close your eyes and picture the moment you learned of your diagnosis. Where were you? What were you doing? Where was Jesus? In Scripture, God tells us repeatedly that He is *always* with us (Isaiah 41:10; Jeremiah 1:8; Joshua 1:9; Matthew 28:20). If you didn't see Him there with you before, close your eyes and look for Him there now. What was He doing?

2. Meditate on the picture you see. Ask the Holy Spirit to speak to you. Listen carefully, take your time. Remember, the Spirit of God is always encouraging. If you're hearing negative thoughts, it's not from Him, so skip to #3.

3. Read Psalm 27:1-14 to encourage your heart.

2

His Compassion

*Praise be to the God and Father of our Lord
Jesus Christ, the Father of compassion
and the God of all comfort.*

2 Corinthians 1:3

I received the diagnosis on a beautiful summer afternoon while at a friend's house swimming with the
kids. It was a pleasant distraction from the phone call
I was awaiting. I hadn't told my friend what was happening because she was prone to worrying. I was a little
anxious but truly believed the lump would be benign.
As the afternoon ended, I gathered our belongings and
rounded up the kids. I had just packed the car and was
walking across the lawn to say goodbye when my phone
rang. It was my doctor with the news. She told me the
cancer was aggressive and invasive, and I didn't know

exactly what that meant, but I was pretty sure I was going to die.

The Lord's gracious hand in the timing of that phone call is something I will never forget. If it had come just minutes later, I would have been driving home alone with my children. My compassionate heavenly Father knew that I needed to receive that traumatic news in the presence of a friend. He knew that I needed her to hug me and hold me and tell me everything was going to be all right even though it all sounded so bad. He knew I needed my friend to keep my kids so they wouldn't have to watch their mom fall apart. He was there protecting my children, protecting me, from more than we all could bear.

God speaks
through divine timing.

Moments with God

1. How did the Lord show you compassion in the aftermath of your diagnosis? Perhaps it came in the form of a friend or family member, in the kind words or smile from a healthcare provider, a Scripture verse, a song, or some other form of comfort to ease the shock of the news. Journal the things you remember and say a prayer of thanksgiving over each one.

2. If you're struggling to recognize the Lord's presence in your diagnosis, ask Him to show you now. If you don't receive a response right away, wait for His reply. Read Luke 8:40–56 and be encouraged by the stories of faith and healing. How do these stories impact your faith in your own healing?

3. Tell the Lord what you are feeling right now and ask Him for whatever it is you need. Read 1 Peter 5:7. Jesus cares for you, and He wants to carry your fear and worries for you. He wants to lighten the burden you feel. Acknowledge these things in prayer, and when you are ready, tell Jesus you receive this great promise from Him (see Psalm 145:13).

4. If you are not up for these exercises now, stay open to how God might lead you here later. Healing is not a formula. There is no right or wrong way to seek God.

3

The First Night

Enter his gates with thanksgiving,
and his courts with praise;
give thanks to him and praise his name.

Psalm 100:4

The first night after my diagnosis was the worst. I felt like I was alone in a dark underwater cave with my scuba tank running on empty. The fear was intense. All night long between sobs, I prayed and recited Scripture. Every Bible verse I had ever learned, whether fitting for the moment or not, I prayed again and again. Eventually, I noticed that each time I said a verse, I felt a *blip* of peace. The blips didn't last long—they were truly *blips*—but what a welcomed relief! I thanked God for the peace I was experiencing through the power of speaking His Word.

As the night went on, my heart filled with thanksgiving. I was especially thankful for my faith. *What if I didn't have faith? Or what if I was still struggling with it like I had for much of my life?* What a relief I had worked through the major issues of my faith and it was solid.

I was thankful for the comfort I received from Scripture, and that I knew where to go in my Bible for more comfort and help. I was thankful to be part of an amazing church with people who would pray for me and a healing ministry that would care for me. I was thankful for my husband and family and the friends in my life who I knew would support me. And I was so incredibly thankful for the impenetrable foundation of Jesus Christ to hold me up when my world was crumbling. I truly believe the spirit of thankfulness I received that first night is what opened the eyes of my heart and enabled me to see the Lord's face throughout the rest of my journey.

*God speaks
through the spirit of thankfulness.*

Moments with God

1. Psalm 100 teaches us that we enter the presence of God with thanksgiving and praise. The difference between the two is that we *thank* God for *what he*

has done, and we *praise* Him for *who He is.* Take a moment right now to thank Him for what He has done in your life. If this feels difficult, start by thanking Him for Jesus, who sacrificed His life for you so you can spend eternity in heaven (see John 3:16; Appendix I). Then ask Him to show you one thing or one person who has been a blessing to you recently. Sometimes when we begin thanking God, He opens the floodgates of gratitude!

2. In the Psalms, David wrote, "Let everything that has breath praise the Lord" (Psalm 105:6). The Bible is loaded with descriptions of God's magnificent character. Read them and praise Him for who He is. For example, "Lord, I praise You that You are the Savior of the world. I praise You that You are good and gracious, faithful, eternal, and wise." Praise Him through a worship song or by reading one of the many psalms of praise aloud. Praise Him as if He were sitting right there next to you. Psalms 18, 34, 96, 103, and 148 are some of my favorites.

3. As you enter the presence of the Lord, tell Him what you need. Then sit with Him quietly and give the Holy Spirit time to respond.

4. My encounter with God is a testimony of the power of God's Word. When we say Bible verses aloud or in our hearts, God responds. In my case, God spoke peace into my heart right when I desperately needed it. It's important to read full Bible passages so as not

to miss the context of the full story, but there is great value in memorizing Scripture. What verses do you know? Say them now, aloud or in your heart. Memorize more Bible passages, including Psalm 23.

4

Childlike Faith

*"I tell you the truth, unless you change
and become like little children,
you will never enter the kingdom of heaven."*

Matthew 18:3

The first time I spoke with my pastor about my diagnosis, I told him I was concerned about God's will for my life. He instantly responded with confidence and authority, "God's will is for your children to keep their mother." I thought to myself, *Okay. That sounds really good.* Like a little child who had just been redirected by her loving father, I eagerly received my pastor's words and believed them as truth. My pastor wasn't assuring me that I would be healed; he was assuring me that my heavenly Father *wanted* me healed. In the natural world, a good and loving father would never want cancer for his child.

Like many people, I have wrestled with the difficult questions surrounding God's will and the problem of suffering (see Appendix II). Theologians have debated these topics for centuries, producing a pile of literature far beyond my comprehension. I wasn't looking for definitive answers to complicated questions, but if I was going to confront cancer with faith, I needed assurance that God was on my side.

So, I searched the Bible to affirm my pastor's words and was encouraged by what I found. The Bible states plainly that Jesus is the exact representation of God (see John 14:9; Colossians 1:15; Hebrews 1:3). In fact, the words of Jesus are the words of God (see John 1:1, 14; Hebrews 1:1–2). This means that what Jesus said and what He did reflect the will of our heavenly Father (see John 1:18; 5:19; 10:30). And do you know what else the Bible tells us plainly? Jesus healed every hurting person He encountered! This means that *God's will is for life and health not cancer and death* (see Appendices II and III). The belief that cancer is God's will is a lie that undermines His character. Our trustworthy Father is always good and cancer never is. In fact, the Bible assures us that God gives only good things to His children (Matthew 7:9–11).

If cancer is not God's will, then why do some people get it, and some people don't? And why isn't everyone healed? Why don't all children get to keep their mothers? The simple answer is, "We don't know why." But that answer is unsatisfying to our prideful adult minds, so we ignore it. We neglect the authority of the Creator of the universe and trust our own inferior logic instead.

Our human wisdom is flawed (see 1 Corinthians 3:18–20). Our understanding of our complex world is smaller than a grain of sand (see Job 38; Isaiah 40:12–15). Yet when someone suffers or isn't healed, we claim with certainty, "It's God's will," as if we know.

God's mysteries are unfathomable (Isaiah 40:13; Romans 11:33–34). His thoughts and ways are higher than ours (Psalm 147:5; Isaiah 55:8–9; 1 Corinthians 2:11). Personally, I find that comforting because what I see makes no sense. God has something better for us, and one day the ugly parts will go away (see Revelation 21:1–4). I don't know what life will look like then, but I know it's going to be incredible (see 1 Corinthians 2:9). For now, I'm okay with simple answers to the hard questions because that's what we do for our children: we keep it simple until they're mature enough to handle more. Likewise, as our spirits mature, God will give us understanding about the spiritual things we long to know (see 1 Corinthians 3:1–3; 1 Peter 2:2–3).

We can never be certain about our future, but we can be certain that God is for us and will always be with us (see John 14:16–17; Psalm 145:18; Isaiah 41:10). He has compassion for us and is always available to help us. He listens to our prayers and promises to respond with grace, mercy, and steadfast love (see Hebrews 4:16; Psalm 33:18–20; 145:8–9).

Regardless of what we lack, we have Jesus. No matter how many days we have on earth, we will have Him forever. And we will live our fullest life when we follow Him closely (see John 10:10). A full life isn't one without sorrow or pain or tears (see John 16:33; Psalm

73:25–26); it's a life lived with the heart of a child who knows her heavenly Father is good.

NOTE: For more on the difficult questions about God and cancer, see Appendix II.

God speaks
through pastors and teachers.

Moments with God

1. Have you wondered if cancer is God's will for your life?
    a. If your answer is NO, wonderful! You are in a great place of faith and assurance that God is on your side. Spend time in quiet reflection and thanksgiving for your faith.
    b. If your answer is YES, why? Write a letter to Jesus outlining your concerns. Read Appendix II to probe deeper into Scripture and the questions about God's will, then go back to your letter and process your thoughts and emotions. Tell the Lord what you are thinking, then ask Him what He thinks.

2. We see in the Bible that "hope" is an attribute of God: "May the God of hope fill you with all joy and

peace as you trust in Him, so that you may over-flow with hope by the power of the Holy Spirit" (Romans 15:13). Now that's an encouraging verse! Hope means we believe something is possible. Jesus told us in Matthew 26:16 that all things are possible with God. He specifically said "all things" because He wants us to carry hope for everything in life. Physical healing isn't assured when we have faith and hope for it, but when we walk with a posture of hope, it lightens our path. It keeps us centered on Jesus. Ask the Lord to increase your hope for the things you need. Immerse yourself in stories of hope written by others who have overcome cancer and other hardships.

3. We all get to choose how we approach cancer, no matter our diagnosis or prognosis. It's good to have hope for physical healing provided it's grounded in a spirit of humility. Genuine hope is different from false hope, which is religious-coated denial driven by a spirit of pride. False hope can separate us from the grace of God and foster disappointment. A person with false hope believes, "I know with certainty that I will be healed." A person with genuine hope believes physical healing is possible and puts her faith in God and her life in His hands. What kind of hope do you have? Is it grounded in faith and humility or overconfidence and entitlement? If you are carrying false hope, seek God for forgiveness and ask Him for genuine hope.

4. Read Romans 15:13 again and focus on each part of

it. Notice how it emphasizes "trust in Him" and "the power of the Holy Spirit." How can you apply this to your life and your mindset about cancer?

5. I know from personal experience it's easy to put all our faith and energy into physical healing—but healing occurs in many forms besides physical. It is mental, emotional, and spiritual too. Ask the Lord to open your heart, mind, and spirit to pursue and receive healing in all these ways. If you have already, be sure to journal all your experiences.

6. My childlike faith was grounded in my unwavering belief that God is good. I didn't know with certainty that I would survive cancer, but I was 100 percent sure that God was on my side. Meditate on the goodness of God. It's a fundamental attribute of His character that's central to our ability to trust Him. Read these Bible passages to affirm the goodness of God: 1 Chronicles 16:34; Psalm 34:8; 86:5; 100:5; 145:9; Matthew 7:11; Acts 10:38; Romans 12:2; 1 Timothy 4:4; James 1:17.

5

Today

This is the day that the LORD has made;
let us rejoice and be glad in it.

Psalm 118:24 NRSV

Fourteen days post-diagnosis, I tried to proceed as if life were normal. To distract myself from the gnawing fear, I took my children shopping and allowed each of them to choose one small item. My six-year-old son Zachary chose a protractor, and my eight-year-old daughter Danielle chose a tube of glow-stick bracelets.

The next morning, Danielle shared one of her bracelets with her brother. He ran to me in distress, complaining that she gave him only one. I told him to thank her for sharing and to be happy with the one bracelet he received rather than focusing on the fifteen in the tube he didn't have. As I was speaking to my son, I knew the Lord was speaking to me: *"Don't dwell on what you don't know. Take one day at a time and rejoice in all the good news you have received thus far."* Zachary nodded, thanked his sister, and went on his way. And with my heart a little lighter, I did too.

God speaks through our children.

Moments with God

1. For most of us, fear is a natural response to cancer and there isn't anything anyone can do to take it away. Jesus, on the other hand, can do what humans cannot! There is power in the Holy Spirit, power even to push back fear. I'm sure you've heard the phrase from would-be encouragers, "Faith, not fear." Full disclosure, I want to punch someone every time I hear it because it feels condescending. Of course I have faith, but cancer is scary! Sure, a greater measure of faith can help us manage fear and lessen its power over us, but we can't just turn on a faucet and fill up our glass with more faith! Growing in faith is a process. Besides, the Bible says the antidote to fear isn't faith but *love:* "But perfect love drives out fear..." (1 John 4:18). Read 1 John 4:7-21 which is all about loving God and loving each other. The more we can grasp the power of love, the more equipped we will be to overcome fear. If fear comes

upon you, look for someone nearby to love. A family member, friend, stranger—anyone! In the Bible, "lovingkindness" is a synonym for "steadfast love," so don't forget that even small kindnesses are acts of love. If no one is with you when fear stops by, start planning how you're going to love someone later. Or tell Jesus how much you love Him. Meditate on His immeasurable love for you, and think about all the ways He has shown you His love.

2. Another way to manage fear is to confront it directly. If you struggle with fear of what *could* happen, write down your fears and read them aloud to God, one at a time, as if He were sitting right next to you. Use the phrase "What if…" Now close your eyes and picture Jesus holding your hand. Ask Him to respond to your what-ifs. What encouraging thoughts or pictures come to you? According to Scripture, words from the Lord are always encouraging and life-giving (John 6:63b), so if you are sensing a negative response to your what-if questions, I assure you they are *not* the voice of the Lord. Ask Jesus to silence them. Pray over your what-ifs and ask Him to take authority over them so they no longer have power over you.

3. God didn't give us a spirit of fear. He gave us something much more helpful: a spirit of power and love (2 Timothy 1:7). You might not feel super powerful right now, but I can promise you, with the Spirit of God in you, you absolutely are a powerful warrior! Read Ephesians 6:10–18 and ask the Lord for an

infusion of His power and love to help you stand against the enemy, fear.

4. The Bible tells us to give thanks for everything, always, even in difficult times (Ephesians 5:20). Thanksgiving invites the presence of the Lord, and it also balances our emotions. Read 1 Thessalonians 5:16–18 and set your mind on the will of God. Record all the positives in your life right now.

5. Thanksgiving isn't just about what we have. Thanksgiving, in its most basic and purest form, is about God: who He is and what He's done. Read Psalm 103 and thank God for what He has done according to Scripture.

6. There is no right or wrong way to *feel* about cancer. Every emotion is valid. Joy and sorrow coexist. Even amid our painful emotions, we can *choose* to celebrate "today." Read Philippians 4:4–9 and look for joy around you, even in small things.

7. A pastor friend of mine often says, "Don't pile up your tomorrows." That's a great word for all of us every day! Read John 10:10 and Colossians 2:6–7. Ask the Lord to help you knock down your pile of tomorrows and live in the present moment.

8. Read and memorize Philippians 4:8. What are some of the "whatevers" in your life? Recite this verse whenever you find yourself piling up your tomorrows.

ONE STEP

Maybe it's okay just
to take it one
step
at
a
time
with the faith that
each step will lead me
exactly where
I need to be

by Jai Gaurangi

6

"Jesus"

The name of the LORD is a strong tower;
the righteous run to it and are safe.

Proverbs 18:10

I discovered at the beginning of cancer that when the body becomes weak, the mind quickly follows. Cancer was the most challenging and loneliest season of my life. I had plenty of support from people who loved me, but the turmoil inside me was so dense and gnarled, I couldn't see anyone or anything but darkness. There were many days when I was so anxious, I couldn't even pray. So I would just say "Jesus" because I knew if I could pray only one word, "Jesus" was the right word.

I have met other people who experienced the same thing. When my friend's teenage son was diagnosed with Hodgkin's lymphoma, the most she could do was pace the floor of his hospital room, crying, "Jesus! Jesus!

Jesus!" One of my prayer partners wrote "Jesus" on a slip of paper and slept with it under her pillow.

The Bible tells us to "pray in the Spirit on all occasions with *all kinds* of prayers and requests" (Ephesians 6:18). I may not be a trained religious professional, but I'm pretty sure "all kinds" includes the short ones. In fact, some of my most memorable answered prayers were single sentences.

My first memory of an answered prayer was when I prayed, simply, "Lord, give me strength." I prayed that daily when I was a novice out of college, struggling to find my place in a research laboratory full of seasoned scientists more educated than I. One month later, a new graduate with the same background as mine joined our lab, and he was a Christian. We became great friends, and he gave me the support and encouragement I needed to settle into my role on the team. Praying for "strength" is a simple generic prayer, and I didn't even know what I was asking for, but God knew I needed a friend.

Our prayers don't have to be eloquent or loaded with fancy religious words. Prayer is simply talking to God. We connect with Him—spirit to Spirit—and invite Him into our situation. Whether we articulate our thoughts clearly or not, He hears us, and He always answers us (Matthew 7:7–8; John 16:24; 1 John 5:14–15). Sometimes it's not in the way we hope or expect, but we can trust Him because He's our heavenly Father and He loves us very much.

If you struggle to pray like I did, don't be discouraged. I assure you there will be a time when you can pray more, but until then, "Jesus" is more than enough.

God speaks through the name of Jesus.

Moments with God

1. I've met Christians who long for a greater measure of intimacy with the Lord but are unable to quiet their spirits long enough to hear Him. Some are too sick to engage at all. If you're depressed or work outside the home or have children to tend to, or if you're feeling overwhelmed and just can't hear through the noise, I want to encourage you—it's okay. Being with Jesus doesn't have to be complicated. The simple moments—like the simple prayer "Jesus" —are the beginnings of something greater and will nourish your spirit. Start with the simple and ask Him for more.

2. If you don't feel like you have time to pursue the Lord the way you'd like to, can you think of unconventional times when you can talk to Him? While driving, as you're doing the dishes, or during your lunch break? Ask the Holy Spirit to fill you and show you how to pray. It's not the time or words that matter but your heartfelt declaration of faith.

3. Christian meditation is a beautiful practice that re-centers our minds on Christ and His presence. I've

found many excellent Christ-centered guided meditation videos online. Look for one today or ask a friend to help you find one.

7

Trauma

"If my people who are called by my name
humble themselves, and pray and seek my face
and turn from their wicked ways,
then I will hear from heaven and will forgive their sin
and heal their land."

2 Chronicles 7:14

My daughter and I prayed together for years for little five-year-old Courtney Saunders who had been diagnosed with neuroblastoma at the age of two. Shortly after my own diagnosis, I was devastated to learn that Courtney's cancer had returned. I had never met this precious little girl, but I felt like we were connected.

As the days moved forward, I grew more agitated and hypersensitive to the traumas of other people. Even the sound of a siren rattled me. I learned that I had a form of post-traumatic stress disorder (PTSD) common to cancer fighters. People who have experienced a trauma often relive it through the trauma of others. A cancer diagnosis is not typically labeled a traumatic event, but those of us who have experienced one know that's exactly what it is.

I desperately tried—and failed—to understand how a young child could be afflicted with such a horrible disease. I never asked "why" about myself, but for Courtney and the other children like her, I went straight to God with a litany of questions in boldfaced capital letters and exclamation points.

The Lord's response to me was clear: Cancer is not from Him. It's a consequence of the sin and brokenness in our world. As my pastor explained, disease is an enemy and cancer is very much like a curse. It's not a direct cause-and-effect thing. The cancer I had isn't a judgment from God for my personal sin. If that were the case, we'd all have cancer or some disease. My sin isn't any worse than anyone else's. But the impact of our personal sin does extend far beyond ourselves.

After the horrific terrorist events on 9/11, my pastor gave an unforgettable message about God lifting His hand of protection from our nation. When we as a nation turn from God by continuously ignoring Him, we push Him away. As demonstrated throughout the Old Testament, God will retreat from a people who are out of sync with Him rather than force Himself upon them. God is our loving Father who always combats evil on our behalf to the highest degree possible, but He will not violate the principle of free will to do so. He is sovereign and can do anything, but He limits His influence to the choices people make. Our choices have consequences even beyond ourselves (see Acts 14:15–17; Romans 1:18–25; Psalm 81:12; 2 Chronicles 7:14).

As I thought about Courtney, I felt the power of sin like a sock in the face. At the same time, I felt an infusion of hope. Evil is real, but Jesus overcame it, and He made a way for us to overcome it too. Our hope is in Him alone (Isaiah 40:28–31). When we humble ourselves, confront our personal sin, and surrender facedown to Jesus, our universe and children like Courtney will heal (2 Chronicles 7:14).

God speaks through our questions.

Moments with God

1. Have you been having any symptoms of PTSD? If so, pray every day for the Lord to heal your trauma. Reach out to a family member, minister, or friend who can support you and pray with you when your emotions are triggered.

2. If you are currently wrestling with the problem of suffering, take your questions and emotions to the Lord. Journal them and pray for Him to meet you in those places. Sometimes He gives us answers, but tension is always present in the journey of faith. Ask Him to meet you in the tension. Read Appendix II.

3. We can always seek the Lord's face with a spirit of repentance to engage in the battle against suffering. Repentance takes us from fear to peace because we know that Jesus forgives all our sins (1 John 1:9). Give attention to honest reflection and repentance. Make a commitment to do this regularly.

4. Warrior friends, despite the horror in the world, there is so much hope. Jesus made a promise: "I have overcome the world" (John 16:33). Read that promise again. Our hope is Jesus, and that's a great thing! Read Isaiah 40:21–31, all of it! The Lord never grows weary from the mess we humans have made. He's not happy about it, but listen to this: "He sits enthroned above the circle of the earth" (Isaiah 40:22)! God is sovereign! He has His creation covered. All of it, all of us, are under His authority. Rest in that truth.

8

The Prayer of Relinquishment

*"What demonstrates trust is to put
the thing or the person one loves best
into the Father's hands to do with as He pleases.
Thus, faith is by no means absent in the
Prayer of Relinquishment.
In fact, this prayer is faith in action."*

Catherine Marshall, Beyond Ourselves

As I pleaded with God for my life one morning, I heard myself say "for my children's sake."

I was filled with fear, sadness, and dread at the thought of my children losing their mother. I was overcome with grief, as if I had already left them. But God met me in my grief and assured me that I didn't have to be afraid: *"As much as you love your children, I love them even more."*

God revealed in that moment that my love for my children had become like an idol in my life—a wedge between me and Him. In her book *Beyond Ourselves*,

Catherine Marshall explains, "Fear is a barrier erected between us and God, so that His power cannot get through to us."[2] I love my children more than anything I've ever loved in the world. I've never known a greater joy than seeing their faces for the first time. But my fear for them was keeping me from trusting God, and my healing was being hindered because of it. I thought about Abraham who loved God so much, he was willing to sacrifice his son Isaac (Genesis 22). If I expected the power of God to heal me, I needed to let go of my children too.

With the help of the Holy Spirit, I was able to relinquish my children to God. The heaviness lifted, and I could breathe again. I no longer needed to safeguard my children; God would care for them. Even if I was taken away, He would be their protector. He is their Father too.

An idol is anything or anyone that we put before God as our most important focus and priority. We think of an idol as a golden statue the Israelites worshipped in ancient times, but even today idols are plentiful. Idols are serious business for God and not something we should take lightly. He is a jealous God and expects us to put Him first (Deuteronomy 5:6–8); even before our family. It's heartbreaking to let go of whom or what we cherish the most and impossible to do it without the grace of the Holy Spirit. My heavenly Father restored my trust in Him so fully that not only was I confident my kids would be okay, I believed I would be too.

God speaks through the Holy Spirit.

Moments with God

1. Jesus made the ultimate sacrifice and relinquished His life for our sake. It was emotionally devastating for Him, but He trusted His Father. Read Matthew 26:36–46. Does it help you to know that Jesus knows just how you are feeling? He, too, needed the help and grace of God.

2. Pray for the Holy Spirit to search your heart and reveal any idols in your life. Then go before the Lord with a spirit of repentance and seek His forgiveness (see Psalm 139:23–24).

3. What are you most afraid of losing to cancer? Your job, your independence, your masculinity/femininity, your hair, your quality of life, your spouse, your children, your life, or something else? Be honest and let yourself feel. Talk with the Lord about everything that's been stirred up.

4. When we try to protect ourselves or someone else from something we can't control, it puts a tremendous strain on our peace and our ability to heal. Do you feel this way? Who are you trying to protect? Is your grip on this person keeping you from trusting God? It might be tempting to skip this question, but ask the Holy Spirit to comfort you as you think deeply about these things.

5. Talk to the Lord about what you've identified in the previous questions. When you're ready, relinquish to Him whomever or whatever you are safeguarding. You may wish to use the prayer below or speak to Him straight from your heart. Return to this page later and record how the prayer has impacted your peace.

6. If you're not ready to do this, it's okay. Read Matthew 26:36–46 and pray, as Jesus did, for grace, strength, and courage to let go. Trust the Lord to walk you through the process.

A PRAYER OF RELINQUISHMENT

Lord, You know how tightly I have been clenching _____ to my bosom for fear that I will lose this precious gift from You. While I cannot imagine my life without _____, I have no life without You. So, Father, forgive me for holding _____ in the place of my heart that is reserved for You. I relinquish _____ to You with my full trust, and I surrender my will to Yours even though my emotions don't agree. Please help me stay true to my promise. In Jesus's name, amen.

Spring

HOPE

There's a little bird called hope
that perches in my heart
that sings and sings and sings
even when its branches fall apart.
There's a little bird called hope
that sits within my soul
whose warm and heartfelt singing
makes my aching heart feel whole.
And even when the music stops,
it will beat its little wings
beating to the rhythm
of the heart for whom it sings.
There's a little bird called hope
that will never fly away,
This little bird called hope
has nested and will stay.
This little bird and I can never be apart,
for this little bird is none other than the
Lord within my heart.

by Jai Gaurangi

9

Partnership with God

*"I am the vine; you are the branches.
If you remain in me and I in you, you will bear much fruit;
apart from me you can do nothing."*

John 15:4–5

Prior to my treatment, I did some online research and found a blog written by a Christian woman with advanced breast cancer. She believed that faith in God's healing meant she couldn't have medical treatment at the same time. My heart broke as I read her posts. Her story did not end well.

I have a degree in biochemistry, and I have always believed science and medicine come from God. They reveal His divine nature and masterful creation (see Romans 1:19–20). In fact, the Bible is loaded with references to medicine (see Appendix III). Cancer, not medicine, is the enemy. For me, receiving medical treatment was never a question. The Lord led me to be aggressive with my treatment because cancer is an aggressive attack from the evil one.

Healing from cancer requires partnership with God. We can't do what He does, and He won't do what we can do. He is sovereign, and He *can* do anything, but He has chosen to operate in a way that requires our participation. "Faith" doesn't mean we tell Him what we want and expect Him to act. Hebrews 11 is a rich summary of faith in action. Noah, Abraham, Moses, Joshua, Gideon, Samson, David, Samuel, and the prophets actively partnered with God in faith to bring forth kingdom fruit (Hebrews 11:1–40). We, too, must activate our faith with prayer and action (see James 2:14–17).

The Lord guides us in the process of healing, but we are the lead actor in the play. Prayer, worship, medicine, exercise, nutrition, and various forms of alternative medicines and therapies are all avenues to restored health. Certainly, God can heal anyone supernaturally and sometimes He does, but without clear direction and solid confirmation, the pursuit of supernatural healing alone may be prideful and tragic.

God speaks through the gift of medicine.

Moments with God

1. Have you ever felt that receiving medical treatment for cancer is evidence of a lack of faith? If so, read Hebrews 11 and take note of how the faith of each biblical character was ACTIVE. Choose one of the biblical characters mentioned in this chapter to explore more deeply. Read about their life and draw strength from what was accomplished through their faith-inspired action.

2. What is your part in the process of healing from cancer? What is God's part? Consider the difference and how they complement one another.

3. Partnering with God during cancer isn't just about physical healing. God wants to heal us spiritually as well. Read Luke 17:11–17. Notice that all ten lepers were healed by Jesus physically, but the one who returned to give thanks was healed again—this time spiritually. For me, spiritual healing took place during the process of physical healing. For others, it may come before or after, and some may receive spiritual healing alone. God's healing is a mystery, but we know it is not formulaic. The important thing to remember is *spiritual healing is available to all of us.*

10

Decisions

"I will instruct you and teach you
in the way you should go;
I will counsel you with my loving eye on you."

Psalm 32:8

We often refer to the significant decisions in our lives as "life-and-death" decisions. The stakes are high, and the right decision is crucial. So we do our part, using all the resources we have, researching our options, listening to advice, and carefully weighing the risks and benefits. But sometimes, despite this process, the "right" decision remains unclear, and we find ourselves in a swirl of ambiguity.

As I navigated the real life-and-death decisions of cancer, the quest for the right decision became a quest for the "perfect" decision. So I pushed harder, to be even wiser, more diligent, more insightful, as if heightening my efforts in response to the seriousness of the situation would make it perfectly clear. But my increased effort only increased the weight of the pressure I felt.

I learned that the decisions I faced during cancer were just like the other important decisions I'd faced throughout my life. No matter how thoughtful or educated or judicious I might be, there was always a chance that I would miss something or that some of the pieces would be missing. The best I could do was simply *my best*.

My first big decision came immediately. *What kind of surgery should I have?* Two surgeons were confident a lumpectomy would suffice, but a third recommended a mastectomy. The latter option wasn't my preference, but it was the choice that gave me peace. The Lord is Jehovah Shalom—the God of Peace—and He often speaks to us through peace. So I followed His voice and chose the aggressive path.

Next, I needed to choose an oncologist. I met with three doctors, and two were strong candidates. The man from Harvard was warm and I really liked him, but I was more drawn to the woman from Canada. I prayed in circles for a while, ignoring my inner voice of peace, until I recognized the problem: I had been distracted by Harvard's prestigious reputation. *Let it go, Joellen!* Clearly the doctor from Canada was the right one for me.

The decision about chemotherapy was the hardest. My lymph nodes were negative, but the tumor had grown into my blood vessels (called lymphovascular invasion, or LVI), which increased my risk of metastasis. Some oncologists consider LVI equivalent to one positive node, which would have upped the cancer to Stage 2 and flagged me for more chemo. I was initially given four treatments, but afterward, my doctor offered me more treatment with a different cocktail. I was exhausted—physically and mentally—and was overwhelmed by the prospect of more chemo. The long-term side effects of the new mixture could be severe. We didn't want to pump my veins full of more toxic chemicals, but we didn't want to miss anything either. My doctor presented my case to a panel of her peers, hoping for a consensus, but it was split 50/50. The decision was all mine.

When I prayed about it, I recalled the doctor from Harvard and the connection I felt with him. So my husband and I paid him a visit, and we spoke for a very long time. It was a difficult decision, and he struggled to give an opinion. Finally, my husband asked what he would do if it were his wife. After several silent moments, he said no to the extra chemo, and with confidence in the Lord's leading, we did too.

It's overwhelming to navigate the decisions of cancer. None of my decisions were obvious or easy. Each was interlaced with anxiety and fear. But I got through them all by seeking the Lord and trusting His guidance. I am grateful for my doctors who took great care of me and for the physician from Harvard who brought me to the finish line. All were answers to prayer. I have never second-guessed the voice of the Lord, nor have I regretted any of my choices.

God speaks through peace.

Moments with God

1. Dependence on God is a learning process that begins with prayer. The Bible says to pray about everything, with a spirit of thanksgiving, and without giving up (Luke 18:1; Ephesians 6:18; Philippians 4:6–7). What do you need to pray about today? Ask God to provide clarity for the choices you are facing.

2. Pray until you feel like your prayers have been exhausted and then step back. Give Him room to answer. If you're not sure how to pray, simply say, "Lord, I trust you with all my heart, but I don't know what to do. There is so much that I don't understand, yet you know all things. Nothing is too hard for you. So, Lord, guide me in these decisions. Make my path straight. Give me the faith to follow you" (from Proverbs 3:5–6).

3. It takes faith and discernment to know when our thoughts are not our own but are the voice of the Lord. The first question to consider relates to the quality of your relationship with Him. Do you have one? Is it growing? (see Appendix I). Has He spoken to you in the past? Ask the Lord for discernment, confirmation, and peace.

4. Whenever we believe we have heard from God, especially for big things, it is wise to ask for confirmation. Seeking confirmation is not second-guessing; it's testing the Spirit to make sure it's from God (see 1 John 4:1). Ask God for confirmation. Sometimes it comes through Scripture or a book, a "coincidence," a relevant sermon that seems to be directed at you, the prayers of others or your own prayers, dreams, signs on buildings, divine timing, reliable counsel, or chance meetings with others.

5. If you believe you have heard the Lord for your decision, move forward in faith without second-guessing. If you are drawn to a particular doctor, be confident in their advice and remember to pray for their wisdom. If the Lord speaks through Scripture, then believe and obey. Ask the Lord for the voice of peace to guide you. God is not a God of confusion but of peace. He Himself is our peace (1 Corinthians 14:33; Ephesians 2:14 ESV).

6. How have you grown in your dependence on God so far? In what areas do you need to learn more? If you struggle to depend upon God, ask Him to show you why. What situations occurred in your past that have caused you to question Him or push Him away? Think deeply about these things and journal through them.

7. If you want to depend upon God more, declare it aloud using Scripture as your frame. A declaration is different from a prayer. Try it and let it speak strength into your spirit: "Lord, I will depend upon

You alone to overcome cancer; my hope for healing rests in You. I know that You will protect me and save me; You are my defender, and I will never be defeated. You are my shelter, and I will never be alone; I will trust in You always, in all circumstances. You care about my troubles, for You alone are my God, my refuge, my source of strength. Amen." (from Psalm 62:5–8 GNT).

Do you know the answer to your decision but are afraid to step out? Talk to the Lord about it and ask others to pray you through it.

11

Good Things

You, Lord, keep my lamp burning;
my God turns my darkness into light.

Psalm 18:28

During my surgery, I roomed with a woman named Sharon who had been hospitalized after an emergency appendectomy that left her with a perforated intestine. She was in excruciating pain. Sharon was extremely sympathetic toward me, but her situation seemed so much worse. I was not in pain like she was.

Sharon and I talked whenever we had energy, and I prayed for her often in the quiet of my heart. Just before I left the hospital, the Lord gave me courage to ask her if I could pray *with* her. As I placed my hands over hers, I saw a tear trickle down her face. It was difficult to say goodbye.

Afterwards, I told the Lord I was grateful He had

used my situation for good and asked Him to keep up the good work. It didn't have to be big things, I told Him, but if I could just see some good around me, I would know He was at work.

The Lord graciously answered my prayer, and I saw good things happening all around me. I was grateful for opportunities to reach out to other people, and it was a relief to take my eyes off myself for a while. I was happy to be on a mission for God, but I had to be careful with this. I fell into the trap of expecting good things to happen all the time, and when they didn't, I thought I was doing something wrong. Even the best intentions of our heart can harm us when we're not balanced.

Thankfully, my wonderful prayer ministers at church wisely explained to me that the task of doing good is *God's*, not mine. God doesn't need our performance to make good things happen. He's got that covered. He wants us to be open-hearted and carry our light into the world, but with authenticity. We are meant to shine His light and not try to be its source (see Philippians 2:13).

God speaks through the wisdom of others.

Moments with God

1. Ask the Lord to remind you of the good things that have come from your journey so far, even little things. Are you able to see your loving Father in these moments? Journal them and look back on them to encourage your heart when you are down. Thank Him for each one, then ask Him for more.

2. The next time you encounter someone, whether a family member, friend, or stranger, be attentive to how God wants to shine His light through you. I know it's counterintuitive to think about others when you are hurting, but when you shine His light into the room, it shines over you too.

3. Do you feel as though cancer has consumed your life and you are unable to see good around you? If so, sit outside for a while, or if you are able, take a walk along a trail or path. What do you see? God is everywhere in nature. Focus on all the good things there that He's given you.

4. Our Father, God, doesn't cause cancer so good things will happen, but He does *use* cancer for good (see Romans 8:28). Meditate on this truth. I mean *really* meditate on it—*deeply*. This point is confused all the time, so it's important to get it right. When people say, "Everything happens for a reason," the

implication is that God is the source of our troubles. But this doctrine doesn't align with the character of God as defined by the life of Jesus. It's nothing more than wisdom of the world (1 Corinthians 3:18-20). God is always good, and He always wants what's best for us. Cancer isn't good nor is it the best for us. If this stirs up some questions for you, read Appendix II and the important book *Is God to Blame? Moving Beyond Pat Answers to the Problem of Suffering* by Reverend Gregory Boyd.[10]

12

Guarding Your Heart

My child, pay attention to what I say;
turn your ear to my words.
Do not let them out of your sight,
keep them within your heart;
for they are life to those who find them and
health to one's whole body.
Above all else, guard your heart,
for everything you do flows from it.

Proverbs 4:20–23

A friend of mine gave me a DVD that contained a video of a beautiful international pop star who was diagnosed with Stage 3 breast cancer at the age of thirty-one. I was captivated by her story and inspired by the poignant song she wrote about her journey. Compelled to know of her fate, I searched her name on the internet and was devastated to learn she had died from a recurrence of breast cancer earlier that year. She was thirty-seven.

The experience sent me into a downward spiral as I grieved for her, for others like her, and for myself. Frantically, I called my friend who informed me that she was in my driveway. She had been praying for me that morning and the Lord told her I was in trouble. She took the day off from her demanding job to be with me. She held me, encouraged me, and instinctively removed the DVD from my home. And I began to breathe again.

Cancer is a mental disease. Its attack on the body is physically devastating, but the torment of the mind is the greater battle. God warns us in Scripture to guard our hearts, because what we think is what we believe, and what we believe impacts our bodies. During cancer, the Enemy keeps vigil by our side, seizing every opportunity to speak lies and fill us with fear. Often, we react to fear by seeking information that will soothe us. But when we are in a vulnerable state, the pursuit of knowledge can be destructive.

I learned that I needed to guard my heart by being vigilant about what I listened to, what I read, and what I watched. I learned to resist the temptation to chase after things that would seep into my heart and ruin me. I learned that I needed to be intentional about adhering to Paul's advice: "Whatever is true, whatever is noble, whatever is right, whatever is pure, whatever is lovely, whatever is admirable—if anything is excellent or praiseworthy—think about such things" (Philippians 4:8).

God speaks through friends.

Moments with God

1. On a slip of paper, write down any negative thoughts, memories, or feelings that have been triggered by what you've heard or read. Now exchange them for the love of Christ. Hold the slip of paper in your cupped hands, and ask the Lord to take the words from your mind and replace them with *His words* of truth. Then tear up the piece of paper and throw it away. You may have to do this more than once, but I can tell you from experience that it's an extremely powerful way to release mental anguish in a physical way.

2. As Christ empties your mind of destructive thoughts and memories, you will need to replace the space with something else. The Word of God is the sword of the Spirit and is ready to battle for your mind (Ephesians 6:17). Memorize this verse and recite it when you need a defender (I like the simplified phrasing of the RSV): "Thou shalt keep in perfect peace whose mind is stayed on thee" (Isaiah 26:3). Perhaps you have a different verse ready to stand guard.

3. Read Ephesians 6:10–18 and learn how to clothe yourself with the armor of God. It's an extremely powerful passage in the Bible, so study it!

4. Recite additional Bible verses such as the ones below to help with specific issues you struggle with:

HOPE: "Those who hope in the LORD will renew their strength. They will soar on wings like eagles; they will run and not grow weary; they will walk and not be faint" (Isaiah 40:31).

FAITH: "Everything is possible for one who believes" (Mark 9:23).

PEACE: "I have told you these things, so that in me you may have peace. In this world you will have trouble. But take heart! I have overcome the world" (John 16:33).

TRUST: "When I am afraid, I put my trust in you" (Psalm 56:3).

GRACE: "My grace is sufficient for you, for my power is made perfect in weakness" (2 Corinthians 12:9).

REST: "Be still and know that I am God" (Psalm 46:10).

JOY: The joy of the Lord is [my] strength" (Nehemiah 8:10).

13

Grace

Let us then approach God's throne of grace
with confidence,
so that we may receive mercy and
find grace to help us in our time of need.

Hebrews 4:16

A few weeks into treatment, I sat in church one Sunday morning, physically present but spiritually numb. Chemotherapy had exhausted my energy, and my stores were empty. Out of the blue, a Scripture verse popped into my head: "My grace is sufficient for you, for my power is made perfect in weakness" (2 Corinthians 12:9). I had heard that familiar verse a hundred times, but when I heard it at that moment, I knew God was speaking to me, and I knew exactly what He was saying.

Chemotherapy had made me weak, but I desperately wanted to be strong. I tried with every fiber of my being to fight the weakness but it didn't work, and I became depressed. God showed me in that moment that He didn't want me to fight the weakness. He wanted me weak. He was humbling me and emptying me of myself.

We tend to hold ourselves hostage to a misguided perception of what it means to overcome cancer: "Stay strong." "Fight." "Keep positive." "Have faith." Often, though, our mental push against cancer does nothing but pull us away from God. When we lock our mental pain inside us, it has nowhere to go but deep into our bones and seed the dark of depression. What we can do instead is surrender control of what we can't control to the One who has the power to help us.

For me, surrendering to God meant giving Him control over the areas of my life cancer had invaded: my body, my emotions, my energy, my responsibilities. I trusted God—provided He made us both look good. While my body needed an infusion of medicine, my spirit needed an infusion of grace.

Grace* is something we don't deserve, yet God heaps it upon our plates anyway because He's generous and merciful and He loves us so much. Grace never runs out, but we have to make space for it. Pride consumes our grace-starved space. It urges us to breathe in when we need to breathe out. It feeds our fear of "letting go." It's scary to let go of our emotions—to risk falling apart—but if we don't, we're lying to ourselves and everyone around us. Pride is a sin, and it blocks God's power to heal us: "God opposes the proud but gives grace to the

---

* A broad definition of grace is "the unmerited favor and kindness of God toward man."

humble" (James 4:6 ESV). We need God's grace to cope with cancer honestly.

When the Lord offered me His grace that morning in church, I chose the strength of my gentle Father over the lie of pride. I was tired of fighting—of beating myself up for not dealing with cancer the way I thought I should. I accepted the reality that weakness and sadness are part of the process, and I didn't have to run from those parts. Grace is like God saying, *"It's okay, I've got you; let's do this together."*

God speaks Scripture
directly into our spirit.

Moments with God

1. Cancer can be dark and depressing. I learned early on in my healing process that when our body becomes weak, our mind tends to follow. Have your greatest challenges been physical or mental-emotional or both? As you consider this, journal your thoughts or talk to the Lord about what you are feeling.

2. When we hold onto unrealistic expectations of how we should deal with cancer, we create a barrier to God's grace. What expectations do you have that are

pushing Him away? What do you need to let go of? Ask the Lord to search your heart. Ask Him to reveal whatever fear, burden, or pride you're carrying that may be obstructing His grace. Pray using the words from Psalm 139:23–24: "Search me, God, and know my heart; test me and know my anxious thoughts. See if there is any offensive way in me, and lead me in the way everlasting." What is the Holy Spirit saying to you?

3. Ask the Lord to give you the grace you need *today*; then ask Him again every day.

4. While cancer as we know it is a potentially deadly disease, depression is cancer of the mind and can be just as deadly. If you are experiencing depression, please do not isolate yourself; you do *not* have to do this alone. Reach out to a friend, family member, pastor, or counselor. I reached out to all of those, and it made all the difference.

SURRENDER

It only takes a single
sigh of surrender in a moment
of emotional fatigue
to remember that in those
tender moments of defeat
where every ounce of prestige
is renounced at Your feet
and every layer of pride
is peeled back to reveal
the very essence of our existence
that's when grace
will come to save me
catching me before
I fall into despair
and holding me tightly
in the arms of my prayer

by Jai Gaurangi

14

Resting in His Shadow

Whoever dwells in the shelter of the Most High
will rest in the shadow of the Almighty.

Psalm 91:1

When we're in the middle of turmoil, all we can think about is getting through it. We just want it to end. But the reality of cancer is that it never really ends because we know it might come back. For some, it *has* come back.

How do we live with uncertainty and the blinding reality that life is fragile and completely out of our control? I once heard it described as living in the shadow of death. That certainly is an accurate description of how cancer feels, but I hated it! I told God I did not want to live my life in the shadow of death. So God, in His infinite love and mercy, gave me Psalm 91.

Psalm 91 is a popular psalm, and I'm not sure

how I missed it, but until one day in the middle of chemotherapy, I don't recall having read it. I was sitting in my chair feeling down and beat up when I noticed my Bible, open on my footstool. I placed it on my lap, and there was Psalm 91. I read it and wept. Every sentence on the page was written for me. The Scripture assures us that God is always with us, but in those moments when we *feel* Him close—well, *that's* an encounter in His presence.

"Whoever dwells in the shelter of the Most High will rest in the shadow of the Almighty" (Psalm 91:1). God was telling me that I didn't have to live in the shadow of death. I could rest in *His shadow* instead! What a comforting revelation. I asked God to teach me how to live in His presence under His protection and care, and felt confident that He would, but the rest of the psalm was a little trickier.

I wanted Him to save me from the deadly pestilence that had invaded my life (v. 3), and I longed to be free from the fears that haunted me during the night (v. 5). I was tired of Satan stalking me all day long with his tormenting lies that pierced my hope like arrows (vv. 5–6). I wanted to believe that death would not come near me (v. 7) and that disaster would not come to my family (v. 10). I wanted to believe that God would send His angels to rescue me (v. 11) and that I would have a long life (v. 16), but believing those things was not automatic. I was hopeful for them and wanted to claim them as promises for my life, and while I sensed God wanted them for me too—after all, He had literally dropped the psalm into my lap—I needed confirmation that it was not just my imagination.

With the help of my pastor, I learned how to test the promises that God spoke to me through that psalm. My pastor warned me that there would be no artificial way to expedite the process or rely on the energy of the flesh. It must all flow out of my relationship with God by the power of the Holy Spirit.

First, I was to ask the Lord for what He was promising by praying the psalm back to Him in petition and request: "Lord, would you save me from the fowler's snare and from the deadly pestilence." This would start me out in a place of humility, which is where faith can truly operate. Then, if the Lord was really in the process—if the promise was really from God—the time would come when my faith would rise to the level of claiming it, and I would shift my prayer into a declaration: "Lord, surely You will save me from the fowler's snare and from the deadly pestilence." Then would come another shift when I could thank God for the matter before it had literally come forth: "Thank you, Lord, for saving me from the fowler's snare and from the deadly pestilence." Knowing when to shift was an inward sense. If I tried to move forward too soon, my prayers felt weak and insincere, so I returned to the language that seemed true and right and waited for the Holy Spirit to lead me to the next level.

As I prayed through Psalm 91—sometimes aloud but mostly in the quiet of my heart—I quickly recognized the need for patience and perseverance. I made a commitment to the process because I was committed to

God, and I was convinced He wanted to speak to me through that psalm.

When I was diagnosed, my focus had been completely on physical healing. I didn't care if a part of my body had to be sacrificed. My priority was singular: to LIVE. But the healing God wanted for me was more than physical. An emotional cancer was rooted in my heart, and it was growing fast. It wasn't just my body that was in danger; my mind was a serious threat to my well-being.

Through Psalm 91, the Lord revealed destructive patterns of thinking and bitter roots of judgment. He led me into a time of repentance and helped me forgive others and forgive myself. He helped me tear down walls I had subconsciously built to protect myself from emotional pain and the fear of rejection. He taught me how to receive care from others without apologizing for the inconvenience or carrying guilt. He put dreams on my heart and supplied the hope to realize them. He taught me how to live each day fully for Him rather than dwelling on the number of days I had left on earth.

After an intense six-month season of seeking God through prayer, worship, journaling, reading Scripture, and receiving healing prayer from others, the Lord released the promises He spoke to me through Psalm 91. Many of the stories in this book are testimonies of those promises.

It's humbling to acknowledge our vulnerability and brokenness. It's humbling to say, "I am hurting, and I can't do this on my own." But that's the definition of surrender, and it's what pleases God the most.

Praying through a psalm is not a formula for healing. There is no formula in Scripture; it's a relational dynamic. God met with me in Psalm 91, but He will likely meet with you in a different way. Whether it's in the Bible, a dream, a waterfall, a song, or something else, He will manifest His presence in ways that are uniquely for *you*. Look for the Lord always, and when you see Him, don't let go.

God speaks through the Bible.

Moments with God

1. It may take time for you to learn how to live in the shadow of the Almighty and will likely require a process, as it did for me. Be patient. Persevere. As in any relationship, time together is essential. If you're short on time or energy, make the most of every minute. Time with God doesn't have to be formal. He is always with you, waiting for your attention. Be mindful of His presence in the moment. Driving, folding laundry…He is there.

2. Do you have a favorite psalm? If so, go there now. If not, Psalms 18, 30, 42, 63, 121, and 139 are beautiful entry points into His rest. Read one and meditate on what captivates you, or choose another

passage or book in the Bible and see what jumps out.

3. If you're an artist, reflect on a psalm or Scripture passage, and sketch or paint what He shows you.

4. God loves to speak to us through His creation, so take a walk or hike in the woods or go for a jog and look for Him all around you. If you set your mind on seeking the Lord's presence, you can find Him anywhere. "For, since the creation of the world, God's invisible qualities—His eternal power and divine nature—are made visible, understood from what has been made, so that people are without excuse" (Romans 1:20).

15

The Power of Prayer

*The prayer of a righteous person is
powerful and effective.*

James 5:16

Prior to my postoperative appointment with my surgeon, I found an irregular-looking mole on my elbow. When I asked my surgeon about it, she was concerned and suggested I have it looked at right away. Not the response I had hoped for.

I jumped in my car and dialed the number for directory assistance to get my dermatologist's phone number (this was before the day of smartphones). I didn't want to endure the long trip home before trying to schedule an appointment. The number was available—I had found it before—but the operator couldn't locate it. I tried to avert panic as I got on the highway, but my heart beat faster than I could drive (which, if you know me, is *fast*). Then, the song "Living on a Prayer" came on the radio, and I realized I had forgotten to pray. So I asked God to intervene in my situation.

It was late Friday afternoon, and I knew I would probably have to wait until after the weekend to be seen. My heart sank. Then I realized I would be driving right past my dermatologist's office; maybe I could stop in and maybe— *just maybe*—they would see me today! I knew this was a long shot because my dermatologist is top notch in our state, and it normally takes months to get an appointment. I thanked God for the hope I felt and asked for His mercy. As I pulled into the parking lot, still praying, the song "In the Arms of an Angel" came on the radio. I broke down in tears. I knew I would be seen.

The receptionist was extremely kind and sympathetic to my situation and said she would see what she could do. Moments later she came back. Yes, they would squeeze me in!

Thank you, Lord, for this miracle.

The physician assistant examined me and concluded it could be nothing, it could be atypical, or it could be melanoma. My options were to have a plastic surgeon remove it later, or she could remove it right then even though it would leave a huge scar. She informed me that breast cancer patients have a higher incidence of skin cancer so, as you can guess, I chose the scar. I would need to wait a week for the biopsy results.

I drove home filled with joy and peace, thanking God for His merciful gift. But as the weekend progressed and I anticipated the report, I was tempted by fear once again. I felt like I was on a roller coaster stalled upside down. I didn't understand why this was happening to me now. Hadn't I already been through enough? Rapid-fire questions bombarded my brain. So I did what I knew best: I prayed.

I got on my knees and cried out to my heavenly Father, who gently plucked me from that wretched roller-coaster ride and placed me in His pocket of peace. I knew the biopsy would be negative, and it was!

God speaks through songs.

Moments with God

1. Record a memory of how the Lord answered one of your prayers during cancer. If you can't think of anything, note one of your current prayer requests and come back later to record His response.

2. Sometimes it feels like our prayers aren't answered, at least not in the way we hope, but the Bible assures us God hears every prayer and they all matter. Read James 5:16; 1 Peter 3:12; Jeremiah 29:12; and Psalm 66:17–20. Notice how repentance is an attribute of answered prayer. Reflect on a prayer you believe went unanswered and be honest with Him about how you are feeling about it.

3. Are your prayers in alignment with the Bible? God will never answer a prayer that contradicts what He says in Scripture (see James 4:3). Sometimes the answers to our prayers are already written in the Bible—be sure to check there first.

4. It's impossible to understand the mystery of prayer, but we know our perspective is limited. God has a view that we don't. He has a plan we don't understand (see Isaiah 55:9–11). Your challenge right now is to trust Him and trust what Jesus taught us in Scripture: pray persistently about everything, with whatever measure of faith we have in the moment (Mark 11:24; Ephesians 6:18). Ask Him to protect you from discouragement and to hold steady your faith in the power of prayer. Remember to always pray with thanksgiving and a spirit of repentance.

5. I find great comfort in the truth that Jesus and the Holy Spirit pray for me! Read these Bible verses and let them encourage your heart: Romans 8:26–27, 34; Hebrews 7:25.

6. Read how the Lord answered Hannah's prayer and how she responded with praise, thanksgiving, and honor of her promise (1 Samuel 1:10–2:11).

7. Memorize Philippians 4:6–7: "Do not be anxious about anything, but in every situation, by prayer and petition, with thanksgiving, present your requests to God. And the peace of God, which transcends all understanding, will guard your hearts and your minds in Christ Jesus."

16

A Trip to the Wilderness

Jesus, full of the Holy Spirit,
left the Jordan and was led by the Spirit into the wilderness,
where for forty days he was tempted by the devil.

Luke 4:1–2

On Christmas Day, about a month after chemotherapy ended, I felt pain near my liver. I was terrified that the cancer had returned. Although my doctor was not overly concerned, the fear did not subside. I drenched my husband with tears and found comfort in his arms. Then I sought the Lord for more comfort, as I had done so many times before.

I arrived at church the next Sunday morning feeling completely worn out from the endless mind battle. My pastor preached that "hope" is not the endpoint of a journey, it's the end of a *step* in the journey—that there is plenty of life beyond hope. I loved that! I realized I didn't have to live my life merely hoping to survive, but I could truly LIVE and let go of the paralyzing fear that cancer would return. I left with renewed strength, truly believing it was a day of new beginnings.

Later that day, some friends came to my house, and we had a wonderful afternoon full of laughter, something I desperately needed. Then we prayed throughout my house for almost two hours. It was AMAZING. God's presence was palpable. I was overwhelmed and awed by the love and prayers of my friends. The experience moved us all to tears.

The next morning, I woke up with an exceptionally prayerful heart. I connected with God for longer than usual before I even got out of bed and began my day with JOY—a breakthrough! I was excited about the new faith class that was starting that evening at church. It felt symbolic of the new beginning God had for me.

As the morning progressed, the despair that hovered over me since Christmas Day lifted. I was so encouraged. During my quiet time with the Lord, I received clear direction on some heart issues. More encouragement! A friend surprised me by unexpectedly delivering dinner—an awesome blessing! I found courage to invite him to church, and he said yes. I was thrilled by the boldness of my invitation, a personal triumph.

Then I went to the mailbox and was blown away to find a written apology from someone who had wounded me several years earlier. I had absolutely no expectation this person would ever apologize. In awe of the timing of his letter, I was moved to write a letter of response. After all these years, I had received an apology *that day*.

Also in the mail was a sweet drawing from a little friend of my daughter's. Her love made me smile. I was flying high trying to keep up with all the ways God was pouring out His blessing, exhilarated by all the love I received. As I prepared to take a walk, I was in the middle of a grateful prayer when the phone rang.

It was the Yale Cancer Center calling to schedule an appointment for an MRI. They wanted to be thorough and make sure all was well with my liver. My heart sank. My oncologist was extremely conservative about ordering expensive tests. *Something must be wrong*, I thought. I was caught completely off-guard. Fear slammed me like a tsunami.

Confused and disappointed, I frantically called my friend, who encouraged me to meet with my pastor. He graciously opened his calendar and led me through a time of prayer. I saw a mental image of Jesus sitting with me during the phone call from Yale. He had been with me the whole time, but in the wave of panic, I lost sight of Him. I focused on the image of Jesus and allowed His presence to calm me. My pastor and I sat quietly for a while and then he asked me, "What else?" At first, I didn't know what he meant but when he asked me again, I saw it.

Before that day, I had never been to my pastor's office. We had talked on the phone and emailed, and he had prayed with me in church, but being there next to him in the presence of God was different. I had avoided him because I didn't trust male authority figures. I had been hurt by them too many times in the past and needed to keep my distance.

In that quiet space in the presence of the Lord, I saw the walls crumble. They were walls I had built subconsciously around my heart to protect myself from the fear of rejection. Yet, when they came down, I didn't feel afraid or vulnerable. I felt safe.

My heavenly Father had exposed a deeply rooted heart wound, but His gentle touch didn't sting. He was willing to heal it if I was willing to let *Him* be my fortress.

I left my pastor's office with renewed hope and confidence that my liver would be okay, and it was. I don't think I ever really needed that MRI, but what I did need was to visit my pastor so the Lord could heal my heart.

Christ Himself experienced emotional turbulence during His journey on earth. After He was baptized in the Jordan River, He was filled with the Holy Spirit, then led into the wilderness. There, He was welcomed by the devil, who tempted Him relentlessly (see Matthew 4:1-11; Luke 4:1–2). How devastating it must have been for Him to be yanked from the glorious presence of the Holy Spirit into the pitiful presence of Satan. But Jesus made it out of the wilderness, and we will too. And when we allow Him to touch our pain, He will gently lead us to a healing pool waiting beyond our walls.

God speaks through His presence.

Moments with God

1. Read John 5:1-8. It tells the story of a man who couldn't get past his disability to enter the healing pool right in front of him. But Jesus led him there. And He wants to lead you there too. What internal obstacles or walls do you have that are keeping you from entering in? Close your eyes and ask the Lord to show you. What wounds are hidden behind those walls? Ask the Lord to help you process your pain, even if it brings tears. The process of healing is hard, but the reward is worth the strain. Reach out to someone who can pray you through it.

2. Read Luke 4:1–13 (either now or if you find yourself in the wilderness). Jesus came to earth as a human being with all the same challenges and emotions we have. He's been in the wilderness and knows just how we feel. There is great comfort in that. He also knows from experience how to get through it, and we can learn from Him. Close your eyes and picture Jesus in the wilderness with you. Link arms with Him as you walk through it together. In what way can you "link arms" with the Lord? Do it.

3. Cancer is an emotional roller coaster that can drop us like a rock into the wilderness. If you find yourself there, write an honest and heartfelt prayer about

what's in your heart and ask the Lord to heal it. Pray it repeatedly until your prayer has been exhausted. Remember—healing is a process. Be persistent and persevere. If you don't feel like writing, push yourself. There is power in our written prayers and power when we look back and see what God did through it.

4. Read Psalm 18:1-2 and memorize it. Are you willing to let Jesus be your fortress?

17

The Heart of the Matter

Now the Lord is the Spirit,
and where the Spirit of the Lord is,
there is freedom.

2 Corinthians 3:17

Early in my healing process, my pastor and other prayer ministers encouraged me to look beyond the physical and address my healing from a spiritual perspective. Our bodies and minds are an interconnected system, so our emotions and spirit can impact our physical health (see Appendix IV). With all I was going through, I wasn't exactly thrilled at the notion of embarking on an inward journey, but I trusted those who were ministering to me and committed to the process. Often we need healing in places that are deep and locked in our hearts; places we can't see without the light of other people.

A month after I finished chemotherapy, I joined a faith class at my church. I hadn't really had much energy for learning, so it was an important step for me. I was excited to be with new people in a fresh environment that was encouraging and life-giving. One evening, my pastor prayed over me and repeated the words, "Take the cap off." It was a little odd, but I knew it had something to do with "breaking free." I was curious, so I tucked it away and hoped for revelation.

In his powerful little book, *Once Upon A Prayer*, David Manuel shares how He heard God's voice by reading Scripture passages and then listening for and conversing with the Holy Spirit in His heart. He refers to this practice as "dialoguing with God," and we learned how to practice it in class.[3]

Several weeks after my pastor had prayed over me, our homework assignment was to dialogue with God in the book of Joshua. When I read chapter 6, I heard the Lord speak to my heart: *"I am preparing you, just as I prepared the Israelites to receive the Promised Land."* I told the Lord I was happy to do anything He asked of me, but I would need His help because I felt like I was going in circles.[†]

"You are going in circles," He spoke to my spirit. *"But don't be discouraged. This is all for a reason."*

It's always mind-boggling to encounter the voice of the Spirit, so it took me a few moments to quiet my mind and enter the sacred space of His presence. I asked

---

[†] The Lord instructed Joshua to circle the city of Jericho six times in six days (Joshua 6:3), which is the verse that prompted my dialogue with the Holy Spirit.

Him the "reason." He told me to draw a circle inside of itself, so I began to draw what looked like a spiral and instantly I knew: *With each revolution you are making progress, and eventually you will end up at the heart of the matter.*

I was completely blown away. These thoughts—this revelation—did not come from me. If you've ever experienced a deep sense of awe, you know it's like being frozen in time, unable to breathe, unable to move your limbs, floating in space with a cushion of air carrying you to a place you've never been before, waiting in wonder and expectation that when you open your eyes that were never even closed, you will see yourself face-down at the throne of God.

Thank You, Jesus. Thank You.

In the Bible, the prophet Ezekiel prophesied to the dry bones, "I will make breath enter you and you will come to life" (Ezekiel 37:5). That's exactly what happened to me. It was as if my bones (brittle from the toxic chemicals infused into my veins) and my chest (raw from the incisions that scarred my flesh) had been restored by the breath of God. His promise—that I would discover the heart of the matter—was gold. I could feel something bubbling up in me, and I knew the cap was preparing to come off.

Over the next several months, the Lord led me through the tangled forest in my heart along the path to freedom. Exactly forty weeks after my diagnosis (see "Forty"), I met with my prayer ministers, who prayed boldly for the Lord to remove the cap. I'll never forget the energy in the room. We were all hopeful and expectant that healing would come, and after two hours of intense prayer, charged emotions, and patient hope, the cap popped off! The cap was a *lie* that had been wedged into my belief system like a crusty, old cork in a forgotten bottle of champagne. I had lived my life believing the lie that something was wrong with me. Self-judgment was the heart of the matter. Shame was its heartbeat.

God loves us. Each of us, unconditionally. There is no comparison to the vastness of His love. No matter who loves us, God loves us more. No matter who doesn't love us, God doesn't care. And when we don't love ourselves, God loves us still. Relentlessly. Passionately. Eternally.

Did you know that when God looks at us, He sees Jesus? Not because we *become* Jesus or that we look enough like Him to pass for Him; it's because Jesus covers us with His glory all around us (see John 17:22; 2 Corinthians 3:18; Galatians 3:26-28; Colossians 3:3). That's what God sees, and it's what melts His heart. *God doesn't differentiate the love He has for His beloved Son Jesus and the love He has for <u>all His sons and daughters</u>* (see Romans 8:17). Now, read that sentence again aloud but replace the underlined portion with "me."

On that beautiful day I will never forget, the Lord obliterated the cap that had been holding me back and shattered the power of the lie. God kept His promise. All the poking, prodding, laboring, and digging into my core unearthed a beautiful, one-of-a-kind sparkling diamond brilliantly cut by the gentle hand of God, uniquely shaped like *me* ... the true "me" God created for Himself to reflect His light to the world.

When I left the prayer meeting, I knew I was a

different person. God had healed my body, saved my soul, and restored my heart. It was a day of new beginnings, and I have never felt more free.

*God speaks through
the voice of the Holy Spirit.*

Moments with God

1. Hurts from our past have a negative impact on our emotions, behaviors, and relationships. They create destructive patterns of thinking and unhealthy coping techniques. Often our past rises to the surface during trying times. Jesus wants to heal your body, but He is more concerned about your heart. Cancer may not feel like the best time to address heart matters, but it's the perfect time; cancer is humbling, and humility is the place where faith can do its work. Ask the Lord if there is something from your past He wants to heal. What comes to mind? Your patterns of behavior and emotional triggers are clues to lead you in the right direction.

2. We live in a broken world with broken people who hurt each other. When people hurt us, we tend to hold onto bitterness and resentment. The Bible calls those things "bitter roots," and they are toxic (see

Hebrews 12:15 and Appendix IV). The antidote is *forgiveness*. An important step in the healing process is to forgive those who have hurt us. Jesus taught by example to forgive others even if they don't apologize (see Luke 23:34). Forgiving doesn't mean forgetting; it means cutting the rope of resentment that binds us to the person who hurt us so we no longer live under the power of their sin. When we forgive, we let go of the rope and its chokehold. We are set free from our pain and can allow the wound to heal. If we expect Jesus to forgive us, then we must forgive too (see Mark 11:25; Luke 6:37; Colossians 3:13).

3. Who do you need to forgive? Are you willing to forgive them now? Even if you don't feel like forgiving them, do it anyway. When we set our mind on what is right, our emotions eventually catch up (I have done this, and it works!). You may wish to note the name of the person and the offense(s) they have committed against you, then, one by one, say "I forgive you, ___, for ____." You may have to do this multiple times, but when you have released complete forgiveness, scribble over the offense to delete it from your life forever.

4. When we address heart issues like unforgiveness and lies we believe about ourselves, it's helpful to have someone with us. Does your church have a healing ministry or offer pastoral counseling? Most do, so reach out today. If not, ask a friend to pray with you.

5. Inward healing always requires a process that includes a commitment to spend time with the Lord regularly. Read Joshua 6 and notice all the steps it took to liberate the city of Jericho. Even Joshua couldn't walk around the city once and be done with it; he had to circle it six times over six days, and then seven more times on the seventh day! Our hearts can be like cities with walls that need to be broken down so the Lord can work in us. We can't achieve this by praying once and expecting victory. Ask the Holy Spirit to help you stay faithful to the process and reveal what's bottled up inside you.

6. Freedom awaits you, my warrior friend (see John 8:36). Whatever is locked inside you, the Lord can break through. Sometimes He does it in ways we don't expect, like through strange phrases (like "take the cap off") that don't make sense until we press in and follow our Holy Spirit-guide.

Summer

MEADOW OF FLOWERS

On the other side of fear
lies a meadow where
fragrant flowers array the ground
and an abundance of
only grace is found.
This gentle place lies in wait
for the day my heart is swayed
by a surge of bravery to take
that long-awaited leap of faith.
And as I do, I'll surely know
that my feet will land
where the flowers grow.

by Jai Gaurangi

18

Heart Scars

Then Jesus said, "Get up! Pick up your mat and walk."
At once the man was cured;
he picked up his mat and walked.

John 5:8–9

Words are powerful. They can bless and they can curse. God spoke and the universe was created (see Genesis 1:3-31; Psalm 33:6; Hebrews 11:3). Jesus healed people by speaking life and health (see Matthew 8:3; Luke 4:35; John 5:8–9). The disciples' commands achieved the will of God (see Acts 3:6-8; 14:8-10). Zechariah's words revealed his lack of faith and left him mute (see Luke 1:11–22). On several occasions during my recovery, I was caught off-guard by insensitive comments that called my healing into question.

A doctor once commented, "So the Tamoxifen is keeping your cancer at bay?" *No! There is no cancer LEFT to be kept at bay!* My optometrist asked me if the cancer was in remission. *Remission? No way! I am CURED, as in permanently healed!* A woman in my church asked me how I was doing and added, "I heard your cancer came back." *What? It did? Oh my God! Oh my God!* My internal response to the last remark really shook me. I reacted as if this woman knew something I didn't.

As I pondered these experiences, I was struck by the vulnerability of my heart. I was working hard to believe in my healing, and my heart sank whenever someone challenged my faith. The reality is that after a wounding like cancer, heart scars emerge. Scars are tender, and when they are touched a certain way, particularly with something sharp (like a tongue!), we feel pain. My intense emotional reactions to the insensitive comments of other people were nothing more than a natural response to the trauma of cancer.

When our emotions are triggered by hurtful words from people who mean well, we can turn to the Lord for comfort. He's the only one who understands the fragility of our hearts. He's the safest place we'll ever know. The voice of the Spirit and the words of Scripture are the *Lord's* words to us. They carry authority and power, and they're the only ones that matter.

God speaks with authority.

Moments with God

1. Has anyone made an insensitive comment to you that was discouraging? Tell the Lord what happened and how it made you feel. Ask Him to release it from your memory and replace it with His truth.

2. Read Matthew 8 and 9 and note how Jesus healed all the sick people who came to Him. What do these stories tell you about Jesus's character? What do they tell you about His desire to heal you?

3. Jesus feels the same way about you as He did about each person He healed when He walked the earth. Meditate on this truth. Do you believe He wants to heal you? Draft an honest letter to Jesus expressing your hope or your doubts. Ask Him to respond.

4. Write a love letter to yourself from Jesus and read it whenever your heart scars are triggered.

5. If you have received bad news and your heart scars have become open wounds, I am so sorry. I know Jesus wants to heal you, and I hope you believe that too. He loves you very much. No matter what anyone has told you, we have a God of hope and nothing is too hard for Him. Ask Him for peace and comfort and everything you need right now. Ask Him for grace to live in His strength.

6. There are many Christian guided meditations that are helpful for quieting the mind. Christian mindfulness is also an excellent practice for learning to live in the present moment.[4]

19

The Temptation of Fear

*Finally, be strong in the Lord and
in his mighty power.
Put on the full armor of God,
so that you can take your stand
against the devil's schemes.*

Ephesians 6:10–11

During my recovery, I often took long walks along the rolling sidewalks of my neighborhood to process my emotions. One summer morning, I was halfway into my brisk two-mile jaunt when a domestic rabbit followed me and encircled my feet. I was irritated by the pesky critter who had interrupted my deep train of thought, but being accosted by a domestic rabbit is an unusual event, so I couldn't help but take notice. As I gazed upon the frightened ball of fur bustling for attention, I was reminded that this, too, was one of God's creatures. Someone loved this little animal. I needed to care for it.

I found its home around the bend and resumed my walk, grateful for the opportunity to honor God with a small act of compassion. Inconvenience had turned into opportunity and, with it, an awareness of the Lord's presence. By releasing His care for the rabbit *through me*, the Lord released His loving care *to me.* Anxiety and tension had been building in my spirit in anticipation of my upcoming oncology appointment, but I hadn't even realized I was afraid. By opening my eyes to the rabbit's need, the Lord opened my eyes to my own need.

Jesus met me in that moment and showed me *fear is a temptation.* I had never thought of fear that way before; I had always viewed it as a Goliath—a furious giant with a life and a power all its own. Temptations, however, were pesky irritants I could work around. So I did what Jesus did when He faced temptation in the wilderness (see Matthew 4:1–11); I counterattacked with life-giving Bible verses I had committed to memory for times like this.

Fear is a normal part of cancer that can feel like a ferocious giant. But when we shift our perspective toward the truth of Scripture, fear loses its power. The Bible says that when we are tempted, God always provides a way out (see 1 Corinthians 10:13). The Word of God is a way out. It's our first line of defense and a powerful weapon against the Enemy's antics (see Ephesians 6:17). The next time fear tempts you, think of it as a pesky critter. Grab your slingshot, load it with Scripture, and let the Spirit of God do its work.

God speaks through His creatures.

Moments with God

1. As you read in my rabbit story, sometimes we need a shift in perspective to see the way out. In addition to Scripture, the way out is often a friend who can help us see things differently. Early in my diagnosis, I was told there was a 30 percent chance the cancer would return, which terrified me. But a friend was with me when I got that news, and she pointed out the alternative view: there's a 70 percent chance that it won't! Do you need a shift in perspective for something you are dealing with?

2. Always keep this simple prayer on your tongue: "Lord, lead me not into the temptation of fear but deliver me from the evil one" (from Matthew 6:13).

3. Ask God to show you the root of your fear or any negative emotions that have a grip on you. Is there something you need to release? Whatever He reveals to you, ask Him to help you.

4. The Lord is gracious and does not leave His children helpless against fear. He teaches us how to stand up against the enemy, fear. One way is with the full ar-

mor of God. Read Ephesians 6:10–18, then read it again and again. Soak it in and put it into practice.

5. Read about Bible characters who overcame their fear:

Mary was fearful when she was visited by an angel who told her about the forthcoming birth of Jesus. Imagine how she felt knowing that she would be judged for infidelity. Read her story in Luke 1:26-38 and be encouraged by how she overcame her fear.

Read Ruth 3 and think about how afraid Ruth must have been to follow Naomi's instructions. Read the rest of the book to see how she was rewarded for her courage.

Matthew 26:36-46 tells the story of Jesus and the fear he endured before His crucifixion. His resurrection was the ultimate victory over fear. It is our victory too.

6. Memorize verses that speak life into your spirit and pull them out of your arsenal when you need them:

So do not fear, for I am with you; do not be dismayed, for I am your God. I will strengthen you and help you; I will uphold you with my righteous right hand. (Isaiah 41:10)

Never will I leave you; never will I forsake you. (Hebrews 13:5)

The Lord is my light and my salvation; whom shall

I fear? The LORD is the stronghold of my life; of whom shall I be afraid? (Psalm 27:1)

Take captive every thought to make it obedient to Christ. (2 Corinthians 10:5)

Peace I leave with you; my peace I give you. I do not give to you as the world gives. Do not let your hearts be troubled and do not be afraid. (John 14:27)

Do not be anxious about anything, but in every situation, by prayer and petition, with thanksgiving, present your requests to God. And the peace of God, which transcends all understanding, will guard your hearts and your minds in Christ Jesus. (Philippians 4:6–7)

20

The Question of Recurrence

"Peace, I leave with you;
my peace I give you.
I do not give to you as the world gives.
Do not let your hearts be troubled
and do not be afraid."

John 14:27

I don't typically acknowledge the anniversary of my diagnosis because I prefer to distance myself from the identifying marks of cancer. But when I hit the seven-year mark, I decided it was time. Seven is the biblical number for "perfection" or "completion," and the milestone of seven years felt significant. I didn't throw a bash, but I did celebrate my healing by praising the One who healed me and by sending notes of thanksgiving to a few key people who helped me through it all. And, wouldn't you know it, one month after my seven-year cancerversary, I developed terrible bone pain near my back ribs.

I didn't immediately think of cancer, but it was a gnawing, constant, localized pain that woke me up at night, and since I had never felt anything like it before, my mind eventually went there. Was it possible that metastatic breast cancer had invaded my bones? I've never been one to jump to a conclusion of cancer, and, in fact, this was one of the rare times when an unusual pain in my body caused me to seriously consider cancer recurrence. But after a few painful nights, what else could it be? I tried to think of all the possibilities, but nothing fit. I was tempted by fear, but my prevailing sense was peace. I have learned that *peace* is the voice of the Lord reassuring me (see John 14:27).

I had recently been diagnosed with mononucleosis, but my doctor said bone pain isn't a symptom. Then a strange rash broke out across my abdomen around to my back. It didn't sound like cancer, but I needed to find out before the Enemy launched his arsenal of lies my way.

As it turns out, I had shingles. Shingles?! *Really?!* In the previous five years I hadn't even had a cold, and suddenly I had mono *and* shingles! Never in a million years would I have suspected that the pain in my bones was caused by a rejuvenated Herpes zoster virus lurking in my central nervous system.

The next time you experience unusual symptoms in your body that cause you to fear a cancer recurrence, remember this story. Remember that there are dozens of possible explanations for your symptoms, most of which, like shingles, will never cross your mind.

God speaks through peace.

Moments with God

If you have terminal cancer or have had a recurrence, skip to #5–9.

1. It's normal to *think* about cancer recurrence, but it's harmful to dwell on it. Easier said than done, I know. But the Holy Spirit is your Helper and capable of redirecting your thoughts. Praying Scripture is extremely powerful, so read Hebrews 4:16 and pray it back to God: "Lord, I come boldly before your throne of grace so that I may receive mercy and find grace to help me in my time of need." Once you've prayed from your will, you may feel His grace and peace right away or you may have to wait a little while for your emotions to catch up.

2. Draft a heartfelt prayer about all your fears and concerns and pray it when the Enemy tries to intimidate you. For example, "Dear Lord, I'm so afraid this cancer will come back. I'm so tired of being consumed by the thought of recurrence. Lord, I know that you love me and want me to live out of

joy and not fear, but I need your help. Free me from my anxious thoughts and help me believe in my healing. Help me to live each day fully for you."

3. Journal the details of any recurrence scare you've had that turned out to be nothing. Then look back on your story if you have another scare. Thank the Lord for protecting you before and ask Him to do it again. If you don't have your own story, draw strength from mine.

4. During his struggle, Paul asked others to pray for his protection (Romans 15:30–31). It's humbling to ask others for prayer, but even Paul, one of God's greatest servants, recognized when it was necessary. Ask God right now to give you grace to ask for prayer. When He puts names in your thoughts, reach out to them right away. I assure you that any concerns you might have about burdening your friends are lies from Satan. People want to help but often don't know how. Asking them to pray for you gives them the perfect opportunity to help. Is there a prayer team who prays after the Sunday service? Take advantage of it every week!

5. If you have terminal cancer or have had a recurrence, please don't give up. Keep praying and seeking God with all your heart. He is with you always and will help you with everything you face. Ask others to sit with you and pray with you. He promises to always stay near us and help us, so close your eyes and focus on your breath. As you let out the breath, let go of the tension you feel. Picture the tension in your

exhale. Breathe in life, breathe out death. Breathe in life, breathe out fear. Focus on the sound of your breath as you inhale and exhale. Focus on the sensation of cold as you breathe in and warmth as you breathe out. Look online for guided Christian meditations to settle your heart.

6. If these tools aren't helpful, talk to God aloud. He doesn't want you to feel alone. He wants you to know that He is right there sitting with you now. He wants you to invite Him into your situation and your emotions. He can handle all of them. What do you need right now? What do you need to surrender to Him? Here is a prayer to start:

   "Dear Lord, I'm so afraid of this cancer. I'm disappointed and frustrated. Lord, I know that You love me and want me to experience joy, but I need Your help. Heal me, Lord, in my body, mind, and spirit. Free me from my anxious thoughts. Help me to live each day fully with You."

7. Read these Bible verses to remind you that our God is a God of hope (Romans 15:13), nothing is too hard for Him (Jeremiah 32:17), and nothing can ever separate you from the love of Christ (Romans 8:38–39).

8. Lynn Eib is a gifted author who has worked with thousands of people with advanced and metastatic cancer. She will encourage your heart and help you find peace in her books *When God and Cancer Meet*[5] and *Peace in the Face of Cancer.*[6]

9. As I think about you and others like you who are facing a cancer recurrence or terminal cancer, my heart is heavy. When I know someone is hurting, and I don't know what to say or what to do, I pray. So, this is for you (please insert your name):

    Dear Lord, as I'm writing this, my heart is burdened for my warrior friend who is confronting a very difficult battle. Lord, would you comfort ___ and settle his/her spirit with Your presence. Surround him/her with Your lovingkindness. Put others in his/her path to hold him/her up. I pray that ___ would never feel alone. I pray peace over ___'s mind right now. Lord, give ___ strength for a new day. Guide him/her in every decision and provide for all his/her needs. Father, to believe in You is to believe that You are a God of miracles. I pray boldly for a miracle, Lord. Give ___ victory over fear. Help ___ trust in You alone. Amen.

21

Encouraging Words

"The Holy Spirit leaves no footprints in the sand."
Abraham Kuyper, The Work of the Holy Spirit[7]

I went to church on a Saturday evening during my recovery to pray with my pastor and a few of my peers to practice hearing the voice of God for others. We were praying for the church service the next morning, listening for what God wanted to do. As I prayed and listened (see John 8:47; 10:4, 27), I had a strong sense that someone there would be going through a time of loss that felt like death or trauma. I felt the person would be carrying guilt, that somehow it was his or her fault. I sensed the Lord saying to the person, "It's not your fault."

The next morning at church, my pastor shared some of the words we had heard, including the ones from me: "Someone here has suffered a loss or trauma that he or she feels responsible for. The Lord wants you to know it's not your fault." At the end of the service, I was part of a team who prayed with people at the altar. The last person in my line was a young woman who told us that her sister had tried to commit suicide the previous day and was in the hospital. She was too upset to say much more. We prayed for her and comforted her the best we could. A few days later, I thought about the words I had sensed during the Saturday evening prayer session and realized the young woman we prayed for was indeed experiencing a trauma related to death.

The next week, she told me that her sister was doing better, and while she appeared happy about that, I could tell she was still upset. She told me she felt guilty because she was caught up in her own life and didn't catch the warning signs. I reminded her of the words my pastor had spoken and asked if they resonated with her. Her eyes lit up. "They didn't at the time," she said, "but they do now." I told her that I was the one who heard those words, on the very day her sister attempted suicide, and it was no coincidence she had come to *me* for prayer. Her eyes glistened when I told her it was not her fault.

When I got home, I was filled with so much awe that I couldn't move from my chair for four hours (I'm serious—four hours!). The Holy Spirit is always moving around us and guides us mysteriously at times. The Bible tells us the Spirit manifests in the form of spiritual gifts, and different gifts of the Spirit are given to each of us for the common good (1 Corinthians 12:7). They provide encouragement, instruction, strength, and comfort to others (1 Corinthians 12; 1 Corinthians 14:3; Romans

12:3–8). The words I received that Saturday evening were not my own. They were born from the Spirit of God to comfort and encourage the young woman (see 1 Peter 4:10–11).

My husband visited me often during the four hours I was frozen in my chair. He asked me how my experience that day was affecting my faith in the pictures and words others had spoken to me while I had cancer. I hadn't even thought of that! A woman at my church saw a picture of a sun and assured me, "This is only for a season." Another woman at church had a dream that my son was old, and I was still parenting (there's humor in that, but encouragement nonetheless!). The Lord assured my husband that I would be healed 100 percent. One of my prayer ministers saw a picture of God's hands removing every cancer cell from my body while saying the words, "It is finished." Other people asserted that I would be okay and that good things were coming.

I had faith in those words when I first heard them, but after my encounter with the young woman, my faith rose to new heights. The Lord had given me encouraging words as a gift for someone who needed it; and in the process, He generously returned that gift back to me.

God speaks through encouraging words.

Moments with God

1. Journal any encouraging words you have received from others throughout your life, especially since your diagnosis. If you haven't received any, ask for some! Ask for greater faith.

2. Has God worked mysteriously in your life, or in the lives of people around you? Think deeply about any supernatural encounters you've had and allow them to increase your faith in the Spirit of God. Be mindful of any positive thoughts you have that are unusual; ask the Lord if they're from Him.

3. What are your spiritual gifts (Romans 12:3–8; 1 Corinthians 12)? God typically uses the gifts of the Spirit to edify others and bring unity to the church, but, as I shared in my story, sometimes He gifts them back to us. Ask the Lord for spiritual gifts and watch how He uses you for encouragement, instruction, comfort, and strength to other people (and yourself!).

22

My Trophy

For I am convinced that neither death nor life,
neither angels nor demons,
neither the present nor the future,
nor any powers, neither height nor depth,
nor anything else in all creation,
will be able to separate us from the love of God
that is in Christ Jesus our Lord.

Romans 8:38–39

It's only when we are completely helpless and hopeless that we give our complete attention to God. Cancer brought me to this place. It was dark, and it wasn't fun, but I got to see the Lord's face and that part was a gift.

I spent a lot of my time with God—in the Bible, praying, listening and dancing to worship music, journaling, prayer walking, and resting in His creation. The time with God during cancer was the most intimate time I have ever experienced with Him.

As I recovered, I sensed that indeed this was a special time when the Lord's eyes were on me. It was a time of refinement that would only be for a season. He wasn't going to leave me—He is always with me—but I was not going to remain in the heightened state that connected me to the spirit realm like an umbilical cord. Rebirth would come. This was only for a season.

After my recovery, establishing a new normalcy in my relationship with God proved challenging. I struggled with internal issues from my past that had resurfaced. I have always known that God wants our relationship and not our performance, but as our level of intimacy shifted, I lost confidence in the relationship and unwittingly fell back on old ways of thinking. I subconsciously began to rely on myself again, stealing control of things I had relinquished to Him. And oh what a failure I was!

I feared the consequences of my imperfections, like the people who wouldn't know Jesus because I didn't pray right or my children whose spiritual growth would suffer because I didn't teach them enough. For weeks, I stayed stuck in the cobwebs of my heart, alone and frightened, wrestling with God, until one peaceful spring morning when I met with Jesus.

I had no agenda but to spend time in the Psalms, praising God for who He is. A passage there led me to 1 John 4, and instantly the Lord led me back into His flow of love. He showed me that I had been holding my time of intimacy with Him as a trophy on my shelf, as if it was a once-in-a-lifetime achievement. I was proud of that trophy but fell into its trap of believing I would never have that kind of intimacy with Him again—unless, of course, I had cancer.

Through Scripture, the Lord diverted me from the illusion of that trophy and back into His flow of love. His love was the key I had forgotten and was where I would find grace for everything. I didn't have to fear the mistakes or wrong choices I would make; I simply had to stay anchored in His love (see John 15:5-13). A supernatural transaction took place as I gave the Lord my trophy, and He replaced it with fresh confidence in our relationship.

God speaks through the Bible.

Moments with God

1. When we seek God *purely*—just seek Him for who He is—with no agenda other than to love Him and be with Him, He surprises us with good gifts. Go to God today and talk with Him about what's in your heart. If He leads you to Scripture, go there. Or sit with Him in silence. If you find your mind wandering, it's okay. Don't judge yourself or give up. Gently return your thoughts to the present moment.

2. "Cancer is an idiot!" Have you heard that expression before? A dear pastor friend of mine says it often

when we're praying together for cancer fighters. I love it! Cancer *is* an idiot because it thinks it has power over us, but it's powerless against our faith. Nothing can ever separate us from the love of God. Meditate on Romans 8:35–39. No matter how powerful cancer feels in your life right now, remember, it's an idiot.

3. Read 1 John 4 and think deeply about it. Highlight any verses that jump out at you.

23

His Presence

One thing I ask from the LORD,
this only do I seek:
that I may dwell in the house of the LORD
all the days of my life,
to gaze on the beauty of the LORD
and to seek Him in his temple.

Psalm 27:4

A few months after I finished chemotherapy, my husband and I became official members of our church. As part of the membership process, we were required to share our testimony with one of the elders. I met with an elder on a Sunday morning before heading to the second service of the day. I shared a brief synopsis of my faith journey and mentioned how I struggled with my faith during my teenage years but felt God would someday use my experience to help young girls who were also struggling. The elder said, "Oh, interesting.

An announcement was made this morning during the early service—there is a need right now for women youth leaders. Perhaps that is a role God is calling you to fill."

I glared at her for a moment, then politely responded, "Oh, well, er, I'm not sure this is the right time." Deep down, I was thinking, *Yikes! I didn't mean NOW. SOME day! As in the future. Definitely F-U-T-U-R-E.* I was still deep in my recovery and didn't have an ounce of anything to give to ministry. This was definitely a goal for the future.

I left the interview and went to the church service. When the youth leaders made their announcement, I was overcome with a feeling I've never had before. Little particles of energy surrounded me with an intense forcefield. The energy tingled throughout my body, and I knew instantly that I was being called. (The sensation was much different from the "chills".) At first, I was thrilled because I had never been "called" to a ministry before, and I had always hoped for the experience. I sat with stillness eager to absorb the Lord's presence, but when my brain returned to a steady state, I was daunted. I didn't feel the slightest bit prepared to take on a leadership role that would impact the lives of young believers.

After church, I was a bit bewildered but told my friend what had happened.

"Oh, that's funny," she said. "When they made the announcement, I immediately thought of you."

"Really?!" I screeched. "*Why*?!"

"I don't know," she replied. "I just think you'd be a good role model."

Still perplexed, I shared the experience with my husband.

"That's funny," he said. "When they made the announcement, I thought of you."

"REALLY?" I gasped. "*WHY?*"

"I don't know," he said. "But I wasn't planning to tell you because I knew it was a big commitment, and I didn't think this was the right time."

I reached out to one of the youth leaders, and we talked for a long time. I told her I knew it was a calling, but I wasn't sure of the timing. I was struggling to believe God really wanted me to do this *now*.

The next morning, I prayed. If God really wanted me to do this, I needed confirmation. While I was praying, a thought popped into my head: *"Joellen—an elder, your husband, and your best friend all said the exact same thing to you. How much more confirmation do you need?"*

It was either a coincidence that I gave my testimony to an elder on the same day that a call for youth leaders was announced, or God was speaking to me. I pouted for a while and told Him all the reasons why this was a terrible idea. I told Him that I was weak and empty and had absolutely nothing of myself to give. "*Exactly,*" I heard in my spirit.

When Jesus spoke of our capacity to bear fruit for His kingdom, He described us as branches connected to the vine, which is *Him* (see John 15:5). Cancer had stripped me of my outer leaves —my hair, my energy, my confidence— and exposed my naked branches. Though outwardly I appeared vulnerable, I was rooted in God's grace and strength. And that's the irony of cancer: by exposing our weakness, it empowers the purposes of God.

I called the youth pastor and told him the whole story. Before I could even finish the part about confirmation, he laughed and said, "Yeah, He told three people!"

It was a challenge but a joy to work with the youth. I was way outside my comfort zone and skill set, but the Lord was present through it all. Despite my lack of confidence and credentials, the Spirit of grace empowered me to make one-on-one connections with two young women who needed me more than I needed to be comfortable.

God speaks through His presence.

Moments with God

1. Cancer tries to slow us down, but even during our recovery, God's presence can come upon us at any moment and bring the unexpected. The future can enter the present in a flash. We don't need to have it all figured out before we try something new. We don't even have to have the right skill set to make a difference. We simply need to stay connected to Jesus. Cancer may expose our weaknesses, but it can

never steal our faith or rob Jesus of His power. Read John 15:1–17. What is the Lord saying to you?

2. In what ways have you experienced God's presence? Close your eyes and relive those moments. Do you feel His peace and joy? I relive mine whenever I read my stories, and there is beauty every time. If you struggle to feel God's presence, pray. When we seek God with our whole heart, He promises to reveal Himself to us (see Jeremiah 29:13).

3. Do you feel like you've had to put your life on hold because of cancer? If so, how? Jesus is our Redeemer (see Isaiah 47:4), and He will redeem what has been lost to cancer. Record what you've lost and, next to it, anything you've gained in return. Read Philippians 3:7–9. Journal your thoughts and emotions.

4. Do you have a calling, or are you hoping for one? What do you have that you can give to someone or to a ministry? Even small things yield big things in the kingdom of God (Zechariah 4:10; Matthew 17:20). If you feel like you have absolutely nothing to give right now, perfect. Maybe the Lord has something massive to move that requires a big empty space. Ask Him.

5. My encounter with God taught me the importance of obedience and trust. His purposes run deep and high, long and wide, and in places our eyes are not fashioned to see. We never know what the Lord might want to say to us or do through us. There is joy in all of it, even if it's hard. Keep your attention

on Him *always*, and let go of your compulsion to control the future. Easier said than done, I know, but with the help of the Holy Spirit, you can do it.

GOLDEN MOON

When my hearts' waves
soar and crash upon the shore
I feel Your presence
even more

by Jai Gaurangi

24

Mary

As long as Moses held up his hands, the Israelites were winning,
but whenever he lowered his hands, the Amalekites were winning.
When Moses' hands grew tired,
they took a stone and put it under him and he sat on it.
Aaron and Hur held his hands up—
one on one side, one on the other—
so that his hands remained steady till sunset.

Exodus 17:11–12

I saw Mary in the oncology center on my first day of chemotherapy. She looked about my age, and I could tell it was her first time there too. I didn't feel like approaching her that day, but each time I saw her, I was more drawn to her. For my last treatment, I brought a handmade kerchief to offer Mary. She came in late that morning and it was crowded, so she ended up in the back of the adjacent room, where it would be awkward for me to approach her.

I was fighting a cold that day and soon fell into a coughing fit. The nurse scrambled to get me hot tea. Chemotherapy patients are neurotic about germs, so I was not surprised when the man next to me hightailed it out of there. When my coughing fit subsided, I saw Mary sitting next to me. I chuckled and imagined God whispering in my ear, *"Here, I'm going to make this easy for you."*

I gave Mary the kerchief, and within seconds we were chatting up a storm. We had been diagnosed within days of each other and had the same wonderful doctor. It wasn't long before I mentioned Jesus and she shared her faith too. I learned that her husband had been killed in the World Trade Center on 9/11 and she gave birth to her third daughter, Grace, on 10/11. My heart broke. After all she had been through, she was now facing cancer. I was thankful to learn God had graciously provided her with an amazing new husband who was now girded up by her side.

My bond with Mary grew into a special friendship that was comforting and reassuring. We never had to explain our tears to each other because we always felt the same way. She was my comrade in the arena of cancer, and she kept my hands steady. We took turns holding each other up.

A few months after I finished chemotherapy, my family and I took a vacation to celebrate the end of cancer. We flew to an obscure island in the Caribbean that many of my friends and family hadn't heard of. Mary, though, apparently knew all about it because there she appeared in the lunch buffet one day. She and her family were "coincidentally" vacationing on the same obscure island in the same resort at the exact same time! We were downright floored to see each other.

"This isn't a coincidence," I told her later.

"I know," she replied. "God is saying something important to us, but I don't know what it is."

We celebrated together and watched the five children among us make memories of laughter and joy. We walked on the beach sporting the same chemo-inspired hairstyle, relishing in the calm of the crystal green waters. On our last day on the beach together, Mary heard from the Lord: "He's telling us we have come full circle. He brought us together at the beginning of cancer, and He wants us to be together at the *end.*"

God speaks through "coincidences."

Moments with God

1. It can be tempting to isolate ourselves during cancer, and if you feel that way, I encourage you to resist the temptation! It's extremely important to walk closely with other people. Read Exodus 17:8–16. Like Moses, when we become worn out from the battle, there is no one more qualified and capable to join hands with us, energize us, and raise our arms in victory than those who are walking in it or have already

walked through it. If He hasn't already done so, ask the Lord to bring a Mary into your life. If you already have someone like her, wonderful! Thank Him for the special gift of friendship and cherish it. Pay attention to any "coincidental" encounters you have with anyone.

2. "Full circle" is about completion and can mean different things to different people. Does it resonate with any aspect of your current journey— physical, emotional, or spiritual? What does it mean to you? Read Philippians 1:3–9 and pay attention to verse 6. God always finishes what He starts. It's an attribute of His character. In fact, Jesus is called the "finisher" of our faith (Hebrews 12:2 NKJV). Be encouraged that whatever the Lord is churning up in your spirit, it's just the beginning. Persevere in the process and trust Him to the end.

Autumn

AUTUMN DAYS

Autumn days are for watching the way
auburn leaves fall and kiss the earth
to show that the trees have made peace
with letting go

by Jai Gaurangi

25

The Depth of God's Love

And I pray that you, being rooted and established in love,
may have power, together with all the saints,
to grasp how wide and long and high and deep is the love of Christ,
and to know this love that surpasses knowledge—
that you may be filled to the measure of all the fullness of God.

Ephesians 3:17–19

Before cancer, I knew that God loved me, and I had experienced His love in many ways. But the depth of His love was something I didn't grasp until I reflected on the helpers He sent during my trial. Family, friends, neighbors, members of my church, and even strangers surrounded me with their love and care.

Some traveled across state lines to support me and my family during surgery and chemotherapy. Others cooked meals; did my grocery shopping; watched my children; accompanied me to the hospital and doctors' appointments; made phone calls; took me to the movies and out to lunch; walked with me; prayed for me; prayed with me; petitioned others to pray for me; sent gifts, cards, and emails; hugged me; called me; counseled me; cried with me; held me while I cried; gave me Bible verses; and listened to me. My incredible neighbors filled my freezer with homemade meal-starters. A coworker of my husband made a pink box with the Chinese symbols for hope, faith, and love to hold all my cards and letters. It overflowed.

It was hard for a strong-willed, independent woman like me to accept help from others, but I knew the Lord was humbling me and teaching me how to receive. If I wanted to receive the fullness of His healing, I would have to let others take care of me without guilt or apology.

The abundant individual acts of love shown to me during cancer were extraordinary by their own right, but *collectively,* they were a profound expression of the *depth* of God's love. It was the first time I had been able to grasp how wide and long and high and deep God's love is for me. Those are the exact words from Ephesians 3 a friend had prayed over me long ago. God in His lovingkindness answered that prayer at the perfect time in the most beautiful way.

God speaks through
the prayers and kindnesses of others.

Moments with God

1. I hope you will see from this story how important it is to let others help us, and how equally important it is to support others. If we don't, we may miss out on an opportunity to receive a blessing from God or to let God bless another through us.

2. Make a list of all the people who supported you during cancer and their specific acts of love. Then write or say a prayer of thanksgiving for each of them. Each individual act of care is an incredible blessing, but when you think about them collectively, what do you see?

3. If you don't feel adequately supported or cared for by others, how has the Lord shown you His affection in other ways? Is He teaching you how to rely on Him alone? Who can you reach out to and ask for help? It is humbling to need others—especially humbling to ask—but I encourage you to push yourself today. Sometimes people don't know what you need and are afraid of doing or saying the wrong thing.

4. Do you know how much the Lord loves you? Do you know that He has so much *more* love to give you? If you don't, please read John 3:16, which is the ultimate expression of God's love for you. Here's my prayer for you:

*I pray that out of His glorious riches He may
strengthen you with power through His Spirit
in your inner being, so that Christ may
dwell in your heart through faith.
And I pray that you, being rooted and established in love, may have power, together with
all the Lord's holy people, to grasp how wide
and long and high and deep
is the love of Christ,
and to know this love that surpasses knowledge—that you may be filled to the measure of
all the fullness of God (Ephesians 3:17–19).
Amen.*

BE STILL

Be still my heart
and feel your own weight
for all it implies
is that there's great love
contained inside

by Jai Gaurangi

26

A Day of Salvation

*May the Lord make your love increase
and overflow for each other.*

1 Thessalonians 3:12

In September 2011, a massive hurricane landed on the shore of the southeastern United States and did some major damage. An old college friend lived near its path, so I reached out to her. She had not been affected by the storm, but during our correspondence she shared the news of her recent separation from her husband. I was sad to hear about the loss of her marriage and offered my love and support.

"My husband will be traveling soon," I told her. "Why don't you hop on a plane and come spend a girls' weekend with me?" I hadn't seen this friend in twenty-two years, and we had barely communicated during that time, so when she said yes, I had a feeling God was in it. I was so excited to see her! I asked the Lord to bless our time and provide me with an opportunity to share my faith.

When she arrived, my children connected with her immediately, and it felt like she was part of our family. We went to dinner and talked about all she had been going through. Then she asked me if I would share what I had gone through with cancer. I told her my story, and when I finished, she said, "Wow, I want that kind of faith." At that moment, I knew her heart was open and the Lord had indeed orchestrated our reunion. My spirit flipped into back handsprings.

Later that night we reminisced about our college days, and she went to bed exhausted from her travels. I stayed up for another hour praying and reading Scripture, petitioning the Lord on her behalf. The next morning, I contacted four friends and asked them to pray for her. I truly believed this would be the day of her salvation!

When she awoke, our conversation naturally turned to God, and we spent hours talking about Him. Recently she had considered looking for a church. I smiled at God's perfect timing. We talked about the Bible, my encounters with God, and what it means to believe in Jesus (see Appendix I). *And she gave her life to Christ!* I was amazed. In awe of what God had done. I had invited my friend into my home simply to love her, but God multiplied that love and flooded her heart with a revelation of Christ.

"I feel more peaceful than usual," she said when we exchanged our goodbyes.

I knew it was a sign from the Lord that a spiritual transaction had been made and sealed in heaven. Today, my friend remains a faithful follower of Jesus, and we are closer than ever.

Until I faced cancer, my faith had never been tested. I don't believe that God tests our faith for Himself; He knows when it's genuine. *The testing is for us!* I needed to prove to myself that my faith was real so I could share it confidently with others. My friend needed to see that my faith was genuine so she could embrace it for herself. We are representatives of Christ. When people see our faith, they get a glimpse of Jesus. That's why Paul said genuine faith is of greater worth than gold; it honors and glorifies our Savior and secures the salvation of many souls (1 Peter 1:3–9).

God speaks through our story.

Moments with God

1. To learn more about what it means to give your life to Jesus, read Appendix I.

2. How has cancer changed your faith? Read 1 Peter 1:3–9 and ask the Lord to speak through it.

3. Your faith journey is a powerful story that God will use to draw others to Him. Read about the Samar-

itan woman's amazing encounter with Jesus (John 4:1–26) and then fast-forward to verses 39–42. When the woman shared her testimony about Jesus, many became believers. Ask the Lord to direct your path to people who need to hear your story, whether it's now or sometime in the future. Jesus knows the right time—you don't have to force it. Even a little nugget of your story is worth gold because God multiplies it! Don't ever put pressure on yourself to share the gospel of Christ. Let it flow from the Spirit of God in you. It's up to Him to work through your faith; your part is to share it with *love*.

4. When I had the opportunity to share my story with my friend, it was easy for me to recall the powerful details because I had written them in my journal. Be prepared to give the reason for the hope you have in Christ (see 1 Peter 3:15). Keep your story fresh in your mind by writing it in real-time.

27

Forty

Therefore, we do not lose heart.
Though outwardly we are wasting away,
yet inwardly we are being renewed day by day.
For our light and momentary troubles are achieving for us
an eternal glory that far outweighs them all.
So, we fix our eyes not on what is seen,
but on what is unseen,
since what is seen is temporary,
but what is unseen is eternal.

2 Corinthians 4:16–18

I turned forty right after I finished chemotherapy, a month before my final surgery. Forty is an important number in the Bible that symbolizes a time of need, struggle, and testing. It's a time of preparation for some special action of the Lord. It's a time of grace.

In the story of Noah and the flood, it rained forty days and forty nights (Genesis 7:12). The Israelites ate nothing but manna for forty years (Exodus 16:35). At

Mt. Sinai, Moses stayed on the mountain with God for forty days and forty nights after the sealing of the covenant (Exodus 24:18). Men were sent by the Israelites to explore the land of Canaan for forty days (Numbers 13:25). Caleb was one of these men and was forty years old at the time (Joshua 14:7). The prophet Elijah fled for his life and traveled forty days and nights (1 Kings 19:7–8). Jesus fasted and was tempted in the desert for forty days and nights (see Luke 4:1–2). He appeared to the disciples over a period of forty days after His resurrection and ascended to heaven on that fortieth day (Acts 1:3).

Initially, I didn't notice anything special about being forty during cancer, until the Lord connected the dots through someone who is a big, bold dot in my life. Pastor Arnold from Uganda, Africa, has rescued hundreds of children in hopeless situations, and they now receive food, clothing, medical care, and a good education. This man of God is a gifted preacher, but his persevering faith, enormous compassionate heart, and extraordinary level of sacrifice are what truly set him apart. He has become a dear friend and hero of mine.

Pastor Arnold spoke at my church before I had cancer and another time during my treatment. Both times, he preached the same message in his charming African accent: "Poosh da bay-bay!" (translation: "push the baby"). He explained that our church was birthing something for the Lord. His messages were captivating, and they inspired me to go after my kingdom destiny—whatever that might be!

That's when I realized my journey through cancer

had been *nine months.* The time period between the day of my diagnosis and my dramatic spiritual breakthrough was EXACTLY forty weeks (see "The Heart of the Matter"). The human gestation period from conception to labor is forty weeks! The Lord had my attention— He was birthing something in me. The forty-week trial I faced at forty years old was a time of testing and preparation. My spiritual gestation period was over. I was ready for the Lord to use me!

Cancer is a season when our physical and spiritual challenges are great. Above all, we need the grace of God to persevere in faith. The Lord highlighted the number forty to me to connect my story to stories in Scripture that would inspire me. When Jesus found Himself in strange new territory, He persevered by the power of the Holy Spirit (Luke 4:1–13). When Paul visited foreign lands, he was persecuted but never lost heart (2 Corinthians 4:16–18). When Pastor Arnold struggled to feed 125 children during a pandemic, He kept the faith. God has a plan for the universe, and it includes us. We are His warriors, and like all our heroes—biblical and personal—we *will* persevere by the power of the Holy Spirit and achieve great things for the kingdom of heaven.

God speaks
through numbers in the Bible.

Moments with God

1. Has the Lord ever spoken to you through a number, or gotten your attention in some other unusual way? It's easy to miss Him if our eyes aren't open. Pray for the Lord to awaken your spiritual senses and stay alert to how He might be speaking to you.

2. How have you persevered in your journey and kept the faith? In what ways do you continue to struggle? Ask the Lord to help you persevere, then sit with Him and listen. If your thoughts drift away, it's okay; gently return them to the present moment.

3. Each of the heroes I mentioned was devoted to prayer. Jesus Himself prayed and instructed the disciples to pray (see Luke 22:39–46). Prayer is essential for persevering and emerging triumphantly from our trials. Our prayer times don't have to be formal or complicated. Simple but frequent prayers will help you form the habit. It takes discipline to pray, but when you seek the Holy Spirit for help, your prayers will be life-changing! Make time to pray today, and then do it every day. Pray with all of your heart.

4. The biblical accounts referenced in my story recount challenges the travelers faced, yet each one encountered God along the way and were transformed in

the process. We too can experience the transforming power of God's presence. What spiritual challenges are you facing today? Ask the Lord for courage to confront them and perseverance to overcome them.

28

A Kingdom Assignment

*In a large house there are articles
not only of gold and silver, but also of wood and clay;
some are for special purposes and some for common use.
Those who cleanse themselves from the latter
will be instruments for special purposes,
made holy, useful to the Master
and prepared to do any good work.*

2 Timothy 2:20–21

After cancer, I felt like a new person. I had made it through the emotional battle, and my spirit was renewed. I was ready to serve God in a big way. So I asked the Lord if He would give me something big to do. For two long years, I prayed that prayer. It was a restless time—an itchy season of waiting.

My church prepared to send a team to Uganda, Africa, to minister at the Kampala Children's Center. I always wanted to serve in Africa, so I submitted my application. I prayed about it, but something didn't feel right. I sensed the Lord holding me back because He had something else for me to do. I couldn't discern the "something else." The only things I could think of were small things. I was disappointed but withdrew my application.

My desire to serve persisted, and one day I said to myself aloud, "It's too bad no one at church knows I have project management experience, because maybe they would have something for me to do." There wasn't anyone in the room when I said that. Well, anyone except the Holy Spirit. Apparently, He heard it because two weeks later, I received a phone call from the director of the Uganda Bridge ministry. A choir from the children's center was coming to the United States, and a tour manager was needed. She had been praying for the right person and kept hearing my name. Would I be interested? I barely knew this woman and she barely knew me, so if she was hearing my name, it was the Lord's voice. Evidently, our prayers had intersected. The position required project management experience, and boy, was it big.

Being a tour manager for a children's choir from Africa was not something I had ever done, nor was it something I wanted to do. In fact, I clearly remember the day in church when the choir's US tour was announced (this was before I was asked to lead it). As I watched a poignant video of their performance before the British Prime Minister, I envisioned the superabundance of details and hassles that would likely be involved. *Sounds like a nightmare,* I thought. Being tour manager was not something I would ever sign up for on my own, but the parallel between the God-sized task of the tour and the God-sized project I had been waiting for was impossible to ignore. My two-year prayer had been answered.

It was daunting to be confronted with the life-changing reality of what I had prayed. This project would be all-consuming; but I wanted more of God, so I was willing to do whatever He asked. After all He had done for me, giving Him my life for eight months was the least I could do.

I worked extremely hard to book ninety performances at churches, schools, and businesses to be held throughout New England during a six-week period. I managed every aspect of the tour and coordinated over one hundred volunteers in my church. The level of detail was outrageous and downright exhausting! But when the children arrived in the United States, I instantly fell in love with them. Their performances and personalities were delightful and energizing. I was moved by the impact they had on so many people. The tour was a huge success, and I had the time of my life.

As I look back on my experience with the Destiny Africa Children's Choir, I am grateful the Lord chose me for the task. The weight of responsibility was enormous, but the joy was worth the strain. The greater joy was knowing that God had heard my longing. Jesus always sees and hears us, and He understands our dreams. He answers our prayers in creative ways and surprises us with gifts. The Lord created us for His purpose, and cancer cannot impede His plans (Ephesians 2:10). When we seek Him with an honest heart, He responds in ways that are bigger and better than anything we could ever ask for or imagine (Ephesians 3:20).

God speaks through prayer.

Moments with God

1. Think about your hopes and dreams. Write them in the form of a prayer and share them with God. Then let them go. Don't try to make them happen; just give the Lord room to work. If you feel as though you've lost your ability to dream, that's okay. I've been in that place too. Ask the Lord to put dreams on your heart and trust Him with the timing.

2. Have you ever been presented with an unusual or surprising opportunity? Look back on it now and consider it from a kingdom perspective. Was it from God? How did you respond?

3. Are you willing to let God stretch you outside your comfort zone—either now or when you feel better? The next time a new opportunity comes your way ask the Lord if it's from Him. Even if it's unappealing or you're not sure if you want to do it, ask the Lord to help you take risks. Explore every moment and new relationship with curiosity. Journal your

thoughts and feelings and whatever opportunities come your way—big and small!

4. For those who feel discouraged and withdrawn, you're not alone. Continue to talk to the Lord, and in His time, when the time is right, He will fill you with dreams. Read Isaiah 40:28–31. Then read it again. (It's one of my favorite Bible passages.) Take time to think about it deeply and meditate on it. What is it saying to you?

29

Imperfect Faith

If we are faithless, he remains faithful,
for he cannot disown himself.

2 Timothy 2:13

When the end of my ministry as the Destiny Africa tour manager approached (see "A Kingdom Assignment"), I thought about John the Baptist who had a short and specific ministry and then died. I feared that after my mission was complete, the cancer would return. The fear was intense, so I called on my team of prayer ministers who discerned what was happening in my spirit. My faith had grown exponentially during cancer, but I had put too much faith in my level of faith. I was being tempted to believe that if my faith wasn't perfect, I would lose my healing. My prayer ministers assured me that *Jesus* heals, not my faith.

We know from Scripture that faith is important for

healing to occur (see Matthew 9:22), but not necessarily *perfect* faith. In the book of Mark we see that belief and unbelief coexist, yet Jesus still heals (Mark 9:17–27). Abraham often displayed remarkable faith, but he also struggled with doubt; even so, God credited his faith as righteousness (Genesis 22:1–18; 15:6). Abraham's wife Sarah laughed at God's pledge to give her a child and then lied about her doubt, but God kept His promise anyway and she conceived (Genesis 18:10–15; 21:1–2). God was faithful even when Abraham's and Sarah's faith wasn't perfect. When the father of a demon-possessed boy told Jesus, "I do believe, help me overcome my un-belief" (Mark 9:24), he was essentially saying, "I believe in *you*, Jesus, but I'm afraid of losing my son." I love the father's vulnerability in that story. I wanted that same level of humility to confront my own fear.

It's natural for cancer fighters and long-term survivors to encounter the tension between faith and doubt. That's not something to be ashamed of. In fact, doubt can become the means through which our faith is strengthened. Jesus is full of compassion for us, and when we're honest about our unbelief, He won't allow it to disrupt His blessing. We can confess our unbelief with confidence that even when our faith isn't perfect, Jesus is more than able to make up the difference.

God speaks through our doubt.

Moments with God

1. What doubts do you have today? As you put them to paper, I encourage you to surrender each one to God. Try a simple prayer like, "Lord, I believe, but forgive my unbelief. I surrender ____ to you. Increase my faith." Even if you don't feel like you've released your doubts to God, surrender them in your will by praying as if you have, and eventually your emotions will catch up.

2. Have you experienced tension between faith and doubt? Take comfort in knowing that tension is a normal part of the journey of faith. Pray through your questions and be patient as you seek Him for answers.

3. Overcoming unbelief is part of the spiritual growth process, especially during trials like cancer, but Scripture warns us that unbelief can lead to wrong attitudes and rebellion (Hebrews 3:12–15). Find other believers to encourage and support you if you find yourself turning away from God.

Just. Breathe.

Breathe in trust
Breathe out doubt

Breathe in trust
Breathe out doubt

Breathe in trust
Breathe out doubt

Repeat until you can
say with conviction,

"My Love, I wholeheartedly
trust in Your plan,
and I can understand that
everything You do for me
will only serve to
set me free."

by Jai Gaurangi

30

Kingdom Destiny

"For I know the plans I have for you," declares the Lord,
"plans to prosper you and not to harm you,
plans to give you a hope and a future."

Jeremiah 29:11

There came a glorious time when cancer was in my past. I didn't think about it anymore. If I did, it was fleeting, and my thoughts went to Jesus and the encounters I had with Him. Today, I am healthy and free, and cancer has no power over me.

After my recovery, I sensed God had a kingdom mission for me. Not a temporary assignment like I had received before, but something bigger. My prayer in that season was like that of Isaiah: "Here am I, Lord, send me!" (Isaiah 6:8). Isaiah was not responding to any specific call; the Lord merely asked without detail, "Whom shall I send?" (v. 8). Isaiah displayed massive faith by volunteering for the mission before he knew what it was. I'm no Isaiah, but in a similar way, I was ready and willing to do anything for the Lord. I kept my heart open, believing that if I continued to follow Him patiently, I would eventually arrive at my destiny.

Waiting patiently for God is what I call "active waiting." I took every opportunity that came my way—big or small—because I knew God was preparing me for something, and I wanted to be ready. Even opportunities that were minor or unappealing, I said yes because I knew the stirring inside me was real, and I was willing to do whatever it took to activate it.

Then, one Sunday morning in church, the Lord surprised me. My pastor had just stepped into the pulpit and was about to begin his message when he told me to stand up. This man has a spiritual gift of releasing encouraging words to others. It's exceptionally powerful to receive words publicly from someone like him who has been anointed by God. He told me that while I had managed other peoples' projects, the Lord had projects for *me*. The Lord was giving me an entrepreneurial spirit and would marry my gifts of creativity and administration to bring forth projects from heaven. He prayed for the fulfillment of those projects.

I was blown away! I had never experienced anything like that before. The message confirmed and validated my heart, and I felt like I had just been strapped into the cockpit of a space capsule ready for lift-off!

For days, I was on a spiritual high—excited, attentive, expectant, ready for launch. But nothing happened. Life went on as usual. Apparently, I needed more preparation in the patience department. Reluctantly, I unstrapped the harness and stepped back into everyday life, resigned to another delay, but determined to stay on-the-ready. Then, after a five-year countdown (yes, five years!), I was finally commissioned.

My kingdom mission arrived in dramatic fashion. God spoke in a way that was clear and direct and left no question that it was Him. I was at a one-day conference for Moms in Prayer International (MIP), a ministry I had been part of for ten years. I was fully engaged in worship, and in a video message titled "A Call to Anguish" by Reverend David Wilkerson. The message was about Nehemiah from the Bible, whose passion to rebuild the wall around Jerusalem was fueled by his anguish over the ruined state of God's city.

It was a call for action, and we were challenged to consider our own source of anguish. As I pondered the question, I said in my mind, *Cancer*. The moment I said the word, I received an instant download from the Lord. The whole vision came in a split second—not just the framework but all the details. I knew people who had received "downloads" from the Lord, but never had I gotten one myself. What a crazy-cool experience!

For several seconds I sat frozen in awe, unable to move or breathe. Energy ripped through my core and I realized what had happened. God had just given me my calling—the thing I had been waiting for and pursuing for so long. I was overjoyed but bewildered; I never expected my calling to have anything to do with cancer.

Cancer was in my past. It was not my identity, and I worked hard to keep it that way. Honestly, I didn't want to have anything to do with anything related to cancer. But God is wise and trustworthy. He knows how to refine the pain from our past into fuel that powers His kingdom. With it comes great blessing, healing, and joy.

My mission was to start a prayer ministry for cancer fighters. The structure of the ministry was to be modeled after MIP: one hour of prayer each week using the four parts of prayer.‡ I had been a MIP leader for seven years, which gave me the heart of a prayer warrior and fully equipped me to lead prayer meetings.

I was to pray with cancer fighters and long-term survivors who came to our gatherings, but I was also to pray against the beast of cancer—specifically, to pray for local researchers and businesses working to find the cure. God is destroying cancer, and He's using science and medicine to do it. But we need to invite God into the process or we will never get there. My mission was to partner with God through prayer to activate His plan to release the cure.

Since the impact of cancer crosses all denominational lines, the ministry was to be an expression of *unity*. Eradicating cancer is a mission we all can agree on. Unity is an unspoiled source of kingdom power, and we're going to have to figure out a way to harness it if we want to impact our communities in God-sized ways (see Matthew 18:19–20). My previous involvement in statewide and regional prayer movements in New England had established my passion for unity (one of the many ways God prepared me).

---

‡ The four parts of prayer are praise, thanksgiving, confession, and intercession.

Instead of hosting prayer gatherings at a church, the Lord directed me to hold them in local cancer centers and hospitals. He was breaking through the walls of the church to release His kingdom into the community, another long-standing passion of mine. It was indeed an entrepreneurial mission, a culmination of the words I received from my pastor years ago, and one that aligned with my passions and life's work.

That night, I called my mentor and friend who had been praying with me and supporting me for years as I pursued my kingdom destiny. She believed in me, and she's one of the reasons I never gave up. I told her simply, "I got it," without any details.

For four months I didn't tell another soul about my encounter with God. Not even my husband. I was afraid that if I said it aloud to someone, I would be committed. I was thrilled for the revelation of my mission, but it was intimidating. I didn't know if I could do it—if I *wanted* to do it. One of my mottos in life is "do it or don't do it, but don't do it half-way." If I was going to say yes to God, it needed to be 100 percent wholeheartedly. So I took time to process my calling by studying the book of Nehemiah. (Leadership is one of the book's major themes.)

In the spring of 2015, my prayer ministry was launched at a regional cancer center in Waterbury, Connecticut. Six months later, we secured a second location in New Britain, Connecticut. The story of my ministry is another book, but I can tell you that at the time of this writing, thousands of prayers have been prayed for hundreds of cancer fighters, long-term survivors, families, doctors, healthcare workers, and scientists. We have watched God answer our prayers in big ways and small ways, and every prayer is significant and powerful. I have made lifelong friends, reconnected with old ones, and met many beautiful souls.

MIP is in every state in America and over 125 countries. If you recall, the Lord instructed me to follow the MIP model, and He didn't mention cutting any parts. Talk about daunting! I don't know if such broad ministry growth will happen through me or even in my lifetime, but it's exciting to think about all the people who might experience the power of prayer through the ministry. It has started out small, but the Bible encourages us not to underestimate the significance of small beginnings (see Zechariah 4:10). What God says comes forth (see Isaiah 55:11). What He begins He completes (Philippians 1:6). I believe this book is part of advancing the ministry and reaching more people who need the healing gift of prayer.

It's a joy to serve God and to pray with others—to be a spreader of encouragement and hope. It's exciting to see people's faith transformed when they discover a new way to pray. It's a blessing to be part of something bigger than myself, and to know I am right where God wants me to be. I will never be thankful that I had cancer, but I will always be thankful that I have a God who not only brought me through it but chose me to be part of His plan to destroy it.

God speaks in creative ways.

Moments with God

1. Our unique personality along with our gifts, passions, and experiences are like dots in our lives that frame our kingdom destiny. We define the dots with our choices and actions, but it's the masterful Creator who connects them and reveals our kingdom portrait. What jobs, ministries, relationships, and experiences have you had throughout your life that you consider successful? Which ones have seemed meaningless or felt like dismal failures? What painful or traumatic experiences have you endured? I can tell you with certainty that every one of those is an important dot. Ask the Lord to help you name the dots in your life—the good ones, bad ones, small ones, big ones—and write them down. You might even want to draw actual dots on a page and label each one. Use the "Heart Notes" section at the back of this book.

2. Pray over them one by one, taking time to listen for the voice of the Holy Spirit. For those you've questioned or despised, you might pray like this: "Lord, I don't know why I worked at that piddly little place. It seemed like such a waste of time, but Lord, I know that you can use it, and I trust that you will." For your accomplishments, you might pray something like this: "Lord, thank you for the experience

I had with ___. I pray that you will use my ___ skills to bring forth fruit from heaven." If cancer or another illness or trauma is one of your dots, pray over that too: "Lord, I know that cancer was never Your plan for me, but I believe that together we can overcome it. Redeem what cancer has tried to steal and use it for Your glory."

3. Ask the Lord to connect the dots of your life and reveal your kingdom destiny. I like to pray using Scripture, so try something like this: "Lord, I know the plans you have for me, plans to prosper me and not to harm me, plans for a hope and a future. Thank you, Father, for Your plans! I ask You to connect the dots of my life in a way that only You can do. I trust You, Father, to reveal my kingdom destiny at just the right time. I come into agreement with Your plans, and I call forth my destiny in Jesus's name" (from Jeremiah 29:11).

4. A masterpiece takes time to create. It's a process that requires painstaking care and skill. Artists paint in layers, each one a foundation for the next. All are necessary for the artist's vision to be realized. If a layer is missing, the end-product will lack depth and richness. We may feel frustrated while we're waiting for our portrait to be painted, but the waiting period is usually for a good reason. Sometimes an element of our character or skill set has yet to be developed. Our mission could suffer if we're missing a layer. So, be patient. The Lord will reveal your destiny when

you're ready to steward it. Journal your thoughts and dreams. Pray about them.

5. If you are already walking in your kingdom destiny, congratulations! Give the Lord plenty of praise and thanks! How do you feel about your calling? Do you believe it has been fully or partially realized? Talk to the Lord about these things.

31

More than Ribbons

Yet to all who did receive him,
to those who believed in his name,
he gave the right to become children of God.

John 1:12

Throughout these pages, I've avoided using the phrase "my cancer." This is intentional because cancer isn't mine. When we use the qualifier "my," the thing we are qualifying becomes an identifying mark, and we can even grow affectionate toward it. "My children," "my husband," "my faith," "my ministry"—these are all blessings I cherish and proudly proclaim as mine. Cancer, however, I *despise* and will never allow it to claim my identity. *Not ever!* Likewise, you won't find the phrase "your cancer" anywhere in this book, because I refuse to claim it for you either.

I'm sure there are times when I've inadvertently said

"my cancer" because sometimes the vernacular of the English language commands it. So don't misunderstand me as being legalistic here. I'm not trying to establish a rule I believe everyone should follow, nor am I imploring you to package yourself with a super-spiritual slogan. I'm simply suggesting that we, as cancer survivors, need to thoughtfully consider our identity because the Enemy would like nothing more than to steal it.

I was diagnosed two months before October, which as many of you are aware, is Breast Cancer Awareness Month. I was in the middle of treatment when I entered the supermarket for the first time since my diagnosis and was overcome by cereal boxes and egg cartons sporting pink ribbons. Sure, they represent something good—sponsorship of cancer research—but I flinched every time I saw one.

Invitations in the mail to parade in the survivor leg of various cancer relay walks were plentiful and promptly condemned to the trash. I had no intention of placing a label associated with cancer anywhere on my body. At the time, I had upped my commitment to exercise since it's important for the healing process, and was excited to find a pair of rollerblades that fit comfortably on my bunion-burdened feet. Excited—until I saw the pink-ribbon embellishment delicately stitched on the ankle. *You have got to be kidding me!* The emblem of the land I didn't love was stalking me.

I rebelled against pink ribbons, the month of October, satin survivor sashes, and other trendy hallmarks of breast cancer survivorship—not because those things are bad, but to protect my identity. I am a daughter of the Most-High God, and Jesus Christ is my Redeemer. Yes, I am also the wife of an amazing husband, the mother of two incredible children, a writer, a prayer warrior, and a servant of His kingdom who *happens* to be a cancer survivor. These things are all wonderful and worth celebrating, but they don't define me. They merely characterize what I do and what I have experienced. My identity is not based on my achievements or failures, the opinions of other people, or my oftentimes painful past; it is firmly fixed and established on the foundation of Jesus Christ and who He says I am.

Nine years after my diagnosis, I attended a cancer relay walk to promote my prayer ministry. As I ran my fingers across the satin survivor sash the organizers had given me, I remembered the cereal boxes and rollerblades and how they used to trigger me. But this time was different. It felt okay to join my comrades in the survivor lap, to receive the cheers and encouragement from the supporters standing by. It felt good—even right—because I had learned how to walk in my identity, secure in who I am. Jesus redeemed another piece of me that cancer tried to steal.

If you enjoy the colorful ribbons associated with cancer awareness, then by all means display them. But let's never forget who we are and that our most valuable membership resides in the club of Christ. We are sons and daughters of the Most-High God, and Jesus Christ is our Redeemer who sees us and loves us and is with us to the end.

God speaks through symbols.

Moments with God

1. What words would you use to describe yourself? Write them on a scrap piece of paper.

2. There are many Bible passages and verses that affirm our identity in Christ. I've written a few below in the form of declarations. When we say them aloud, we declare them into our spirit, which is where our perspective changes, our faith increases, and healing begins. If Jesus is your Lord and Savior, declare over yourself the truths below. (If He isn't, read Appendix I.) Highlight the most meaningful ones to you in your journal.

    *   I am a child of God. (1 John 3:1; Galatians 3:26)
    *   I am baptized into Christ. (Galatians 3:27)
    *   I am clothed with Christ. (Galatians 3:27)
    *   I belong to Christ. (Galatians 3:29)
    *   I am free in Christ. (Galatians 5:1, 13)
    *   I am forgiven. (1 John 2:12)
    *   I am loved. (Ephesians 3:17)
    *   I am fearfully and wonderfully made. (Psalm 139:14)
    *   I am accepted. (Romans 15:7)
    *   I am blessed. (Ephesians 1:3)
    *   I am chosen. (John 15:16)
    *   I am God's masterpiece. (Ephesians 2:10)

- I am protected. (Psalm 18:2)
- I am strong and courageous. (Joshua 1:9)
- I am free from condemnation. (Romans 8:1)
- I have a destiny. (Jeremiah 29:11)
- I am a co-heir with Christ. (Romans 8:17; Galatians 4:7)
- I have the mind of Christ. (1 Corinthians 2:16)
- I am God's coworker. (1 Corinthians 3:9)
- My prayers are powerful and effective. (James 5:16)
- I do not have a spirit of fear but of power, love, and self-discipline. (2 Timothy 1:7)
- I can do all things through Christ who strengthens me. (Philippians 4:13)

3. You are special in the Father's eyes, and He wants you to see yourself the way He does. Ask the Lord to show you what He thinks about you. He may reveal this to you over time, so keep your heart open and journal what you hear.

4. Look at the words you wrote on the scrap piece of paper in prompt #1. Based on what you just declared about yourself from the Bible verses in prompt #2, and what you heard from the Lord in prompt #3, what can you add to the list? What can you cross off?

5. Using what you've written on the scrap piece of paper, characterize your identity in a few sentences. Write it in your journal. Remember that your identity is based solely on what Jesus thinks about

you, not what you or others think about you, not by what you do or have done, and not by how you look or where you live.

6. Affirm your identity statement aloud daily until it is memorized. Believe it. My friend, you are a treasure. Thank you for trusting me to walk this road with you.

Appendix I

HOW I CAME TO KNOW JESUS

When I was a kid, I enjoyed Christmas as much as any other child. I loved looking at the packages under the tree, eating my mom's cookies, and the thrill of Christmas morning. Yet after the initial rush from the stuff, I felt empty. One year I remember staring out the window looking for the Christmas star because I thought if I could just see that star, Christmas would mean something.

I often wondered why I thought about Jesus on Christmas, Easter, and Sunday mornings but forgot about Him all the other days. It seemed like I was missing something. Then one summer when I was in high school, a friend invited me to a Christian camp. It was in a beautiful mountain setting, and everyone was super friendly. We had lots of fun adventures and conversations about things that mattered. The theme of the camp was "This is going to be the best week of your life." It was.

That was the week the gospel of Jesus sunk in.

Before camp, I knew the gospel message: Jesus is the Son of God who came to earth as a man to save us (John 3:16–17). He loves us so much that He allowed Himself to be tormented and die an agonizing death on a cross to pay for the sins of the world (Mark 15–16). He rose from His grave on Easter Sunday to abolish death and give life and immortality to those who believe in Him (2 Timothy 1:9–10).

I *knew* those things, but what I didn't realize is there's a difference between "knowing" and "believing." Knowledge happens in the head; belief happens in the heart (see Romans 10:9–10). There was something I needed to do to bridge that gap.

I sat at a picnic table one night at camp trying to grasp what Jesus had done for me. His sacrifice had become very personal. A candle was on the table, and I couldn't take my eyes off it. I felt something I had never felt before. I couldn't talk. A youth leader sat with me in silence, then asked if I wanted to receive God's gift of salvation. He explained what that meant, and I said *yes*.

The way to salvation is two-fold: Repentance of our sin and belief in Jesus Christ as our Lord and Savior. Sin is when we do things our way instead of Jesus's way. It's a problem because God's presence is so powerful that it obliterates sin and whatever or whomever is carrying it. This means heaven is off-limits to all of us unless we're cleansed of our sin (see Romans 3:23; 6:23; James 1:15). There isn't anything we can do on our own to become clean in the sight of God—not even a million good deeds (see Ephesians 2:8–9; Titus 3:4–6). Jesus is the only one who has the power to forgive our offenses (see 1 John 5:11–12). When we confess our sins to Jesus and are truly sorry for them (repentance), we are forgiven and promised eternal life (John 3:16; Romans 10:9; 1

John 1:9). God's forgiveness isn't just about eternity—everything in life is sweeter when we're free from the weight of sin.

My youth leader and I prayed together, and afterward I knew something special had taken place. Long ago, I was born physically, but when I put my faith in Jesus, I received the Holy Spirit and was reborn spiritually (see John 3:3–7; Galatians 4:6; Romans 8:9–11; Titus 3:4–6). The Holy Spirit was what I had been missing (see Ephesians 1:13-14).

Though I received the promise of eternal life and the Holy Spirit instantly, I didn't change outwardly right away, which was a little confusing. I learned that salvation isn't a transaction (see Philippians 2:12); it doesn't come by praying a simple prayer correctly or asking Jesus into our heart. Rather, "salvation is a posture of repentance and faith that you begin in a moment and maintain for the rest of your life."[8] I don't think everyone's "moment" has to look the same. God's *grace* saves us, not adherence to human expectations (Ephesians 2:8–9; 1 Samuel 16:7). When I gave my life to Jesus at camp, that was my moment (see Romans 10:9–10). It was the beginning of a life-long journey of faith with many highs and lows.

Jesus is our friend, and He desires to be in relationship with us throughout our entire life (see John 15:1–15). My personal relationship with Him is what bridged the gap between my head knowledge and genuine belief (see Matthew 15:8; 7:21–23). Like with any friendship, it has taken time and commitment to get to know Jesus but He's part of my everyday life now. I've grown closer to Him by reading the Bible, praying, learning to hear His voice, and relying on the Holy Spirit for all of it. I'm more aware of my blessings and when something captivates me, like the beautiful Connecticut blue sky or when hummingbirds gaze at me through my window, I think of Him and my heart swells with gratitude. When I feel alone, I know that I'm not. I have more joy, hope, and peace than ever before because the Spirit of Christ lives in me (see Romans 8:9–11). It isn't always easy to follow Jesus, and I certainly don't do it perfectly, but I do follow Him genuinely and I think that's what matters most.

Christmas is an important day to celebrate and honor Jesus, and to reflect on how everything changed the day our Savior was born long ago. It's become much more meaningful to me now because I've finally seen my Christmas Star. He's in my window every day.

Moments With God

Recommended Reading: J. D. Greear's *Stop Asking Jesus into Your Heart*

1. If you know *about* Jesus but don't know Him personally, read Matthew 15:1–9, then Matthew 7:21–23, and think about the difference. Salvation is an attitude of repentance and faith that we carry throughout our lives in relationship with Jesus.[9]

The Bible teaches that it comes by belief in Christ, not by being a good person. Good deeds are important, but they flow naturally out of our faith and repentance (see James 2:14–16; Acts 26:20). To get to know Jesus, I encourage you to read the Bible, starting with the New Testament. If you're unable to purchase one, drop by a local Christian church and ask for one.

2. Below are some of the Bible verses that summarize the gospel message. They are an invitation to receive Jesus as your Savior.

> For God so loved the world that He gave His one and only son that whoever believes in Him shall not perish but have eternal life. (John 3:16)

> For all have sinned and fallen short of the glory of God. (Romans 3:23)

> For the wages of sin is death but the gift of God is eternal life in Christ Jesus our Lord. (Romans 6:23)

> If we confess our sins, He is faithful and just and will forgive us our sins and purify us from all unrighteousness. (1 John 1:9)

> If you declare with your mouth, "Jesus is Lord," and believe in your heart that God raised him from the dead, you will be saved.

> For it is with your heart that you believe and are justified, and it is with your mouth that you profess your faith and are saved. (Romans 10:9–10)

> For, everyone who calls on the name of the Lord will be saved. (Romans 10:13)

> And this is the testimony, that God gave us eternal life, and this life is in his Son. Whoever has the Son has life; whoever does not have the Son of God does not have life. I write these things to you who believe in the name of the Son of God that you may know that you have eternal life. (1 John 5:11–13)

3. If you believe that Jesus is the Son of God and want to follow Him, wonderful! This is your moment. I acknowledged my faith with a prayer like this: "Yes, Jesus, I believe in You. I know I'm a sinner. Please forgive me. I accept Your gift of salvation. I commit my life to You." You may wish to pray something similar in the quiet of your heart or with another person. The important thing is to profess your faith in Jesus (see Romans 10:9-10), seek Him wholeheartedly, and get to know Him like you would any other friend. Interact with Him daily by reading the Bible and talking with Him. Prayer is a conversation with a real person who loves you and is always watching over you.

4. Relationship with Jesus is a process, so be patient as

it grows. Faith isn't genuine if it stays in our heads, so allow the Holy Spirit to inspire you into action (James 2:14–26). If you falter, it's okay. We all do. Every minute of every day is new and an opportunity to reconnect with your Savior. Tell a pastor or friend about your new faith in Jesus. It's important to connect with other believers, especially as you begin your new life with Him.

5. If you have not committed your life to Jesus, what questions, fears, or obstacles keep you from believing in Him? Think about these things with honesty. Genuine faith doesn't mean your faith is perfect. In fact, imperfect faith is a sign of genuine faith because it means you're seeking Him with all your heart (see Jeremiah 29:13). Jesus wants us to pursue answers to our questions, but many things about life and faith are a mystery. We'll never understand it all. Ask the Lord to help you work through the obstacles that challenge your faith. It may take some time, but if you have read this far, I'm certain your heart is open. Jesus's heart is always open to you (see Matthew 7:7–8). Whatever is impeding your belief, here's my challenge to you:

   • Acknowledge that all humans including Christians are broken and imperfect.
   • Recognize that a relationship with Jesus is different from a relationship with the church.
   • Acknowledge that many questions about life and faith are a mystery.
   • Ask yourself if the questions and feelings

you're holding on to are worth missing out on eternal life and a more meaningful life on earth.

- Take a risk and let your questions go for now. Wrestle with them later, but do it with Jesus and the help of the Holy Spirit. It's impossible to understand spiritual things without the Spirit of God (see 1 Corinthians 2:14). For now, you can accept the gift of salvation Jesus is offering. I certainly didn't have all my questions worked out when I became a Christian, and I still don't!

- Reach out to someone who can help you process your questions and the verses outlined above. Or visit my website for resources to help you:

www.joellenputnam.com

Thank you for reading about my faith journey.
I hope it encourages you to embark on your own.
Eternity is too serious to ignore.

Appendix II

QUESTIONS ABOUT
GOD AND CANCER

Recommended Reading: Gregory A. Boyd's *Is God to Blame? Beyond Pat Answers to the Problem of Suffering*
Mike McKinniss, M.Div., contributed to this commentary (used here with permission).

Upon receiving a cancer diagnosis, some Christians ask, *Is cancer God's will for my life?* This question comes with a supposition that even if God doesn't cause cancer and suffering directly, He allows it, and, therefore, His hand is in it. But this brings another question: *How can a cancer fighter seek God wholeheartedly for healing if they believe He had something to do with the cancer in the first place?* Wrestling with such questions during cancer isn't easy, but for me, it was essential.

I believe cancer is never God's will for anyone's life. My belief is based on the life of Jesus and the goodness of God[§], which is a major theme throughout the

---

[§] e.g., Psalm 31:19; 86:5; 100:5; 145:9; 1 Chronicles 16:34; Nahum 1:7; Jeremiah 32:38-41; Matthew 7:11; Romans 8:28; 12:2; James 1:17; 1 Timothy 4:4.

Bible. Jesus is always for us! He is the image of the invisible God and the best representation we have of God's will and character (see Colossians 1:15; Hebrews 1:3). Therefore, since Jesus healed every sick person He encountered, we must assume that health, rather than sickness, is God's heart. To believe that cancer and all its devastation is "God's will" is to contradict His goodness and the example given in the person of Jesus Christ.

But what about the "good things" that sometimes arise from cancer? And the Scriptures that proclaim the benefits of trials and suffering? Aren't they evidence that God ordains cancer to teach us and change us so that our faith will be perfected?

Without a doubt, good things can come out of cancer, but it is erroneous to conclude that our gracious and loving Father in heaven ordained cancer and all its horror to accomplish such purposes. Rather, as the Bible says, God brings good *out of all things* (see Romans 8:28). Scripture tells us plainly that our heavenly Father *responds* to evils like cancer by using them for good, but that doesn't mean cancer is part of His plan.

The author of evil is Satan, who is a liar and the great deceiver. He works tirelessly to turn us away from God by lying about the "benefits" of evils like cancer (see Genesis 3:1–6; John 8:44; 2 Corinthians 2:11, 4:4; Revelation 20:10). The truth is, the vast majority of Scripture passages that convey benefits of suffering refer to *religious persecution.*⁵ While some attributes of the various kinds of afflictions may be constant, to suffer for one's faith (often by conscious decision) is vastly different from being afflicted with cancer. By applying Scripture verses specific to religious persecution to broad application across all forms of affliction, there is risk of assigning a meaning that was not intended. In the interpretation of Scripture, context matters.

James refers to the testing of our faith through "trials of many kinds" (James 1:2–4). Here, "trials" point to the kind of difficulties we experience in life that challenge what we believe about God and His character. This verse is certainly applicable to cancer. We are encouraged by James to endure our trials by focusing on the spiritual outcome; when our faith is tested and our beliefs about God are challenged, they either become stronger and more powerful, or they falter. James is merely attempting to encourage us as followers of Christ to trust in God's faithfulness, compassion, and mercy so that our faith prevails in difficult times, and we will be rewarded (see 1:12; 5:10–11). James never suggests that suffering from disease is God's will. In fact, James emphatically directs the church to seek the reversal of illness according to God's will (see 5:13–16).

But if God is sovereign, isn't everything that happens part of His plan? Doesn't everything happen for a reason?

---

⁵ See Acts 5:41; Romans 5:1–5; 1 Thessalonians 1:6; 2 Thessalonians 1:5; 2 Timothy 1:8–12; 2:1–9; Hebrews 10:32; 13:3; 1 Peter 1:3–13; 2:13–20; 3:8–13; 4:12–19; Revelation 1:9.

The statement "everything happens for a reason" implies that God *causes* suffering because it's part of His plan. Conversely, Scripture implies that suffering occurs not because of God's plan but because of a battle between God and the spiritual forces of evil in the heavenly realms (see Ephesians 6:12–13).[10] Pastor and biblical scholar Gregory Boyd contends, "The mystery of evil is a mystery of a war-torn and unfathomably complex creation, not the mystery of God's all-controlling will."[11]

To be sure, God is sovereign, and He *can* do anything; but He gave His children free will, and like every good father, He has chosen to limit His control over their lives. Cancer, like all disease, is not part of God's plan but is a consequence of the sin and brokenness in our world (see Galatians 6:7–8; James 1:13–15). We all experience sin and brokenness, but how or why it manifests into cancer for some people is unknown. We must acknowledge the complexity and mystery of creation and our limited capacity as human beings to comprehend it. Therefore, we can assume that people suffer primarily because the world is under the control of the evil one (see 1 John 5:19; Acts 10:38).

God has given us complete freedom over our lives, but when we as a people choose to live apart from our Creator and reject His offer of protection, we leave ourselves vulnerable to harm and contribute to the calamity of the generations (see Deuteronomy 30:19; Galatians 6:7–8). Those who confess their sin and accept Jesus as their Savior are forgiven, are restored to a right relationship with God, are promised eternal life, and gain access to the grace of God, which sustains us in difficult times (see 1 John 1:9; Romans 10:9; 1 John 5:11–13; Hebrews 4:16). Until Jesus returns to restore the new earth, the consequences of sin and brokenness—including disease—will continue to manifest and take their toll (see Acts 1:6–7; Revelation 21:1–5; Matthew 13:24–30, 36–41).

Yet, we are not without hope! Jesus came to destroy the works of the devil (see 1 John 3:8). God will ultimately win the battle over evil (see John 16:20, 33; Revelation 12:9; 20:10), and one day there will be no more suffering (see Revelation 21:4). Until then, we are called to follow the example of Jesus and respond to the devil's work with faith, prayer, and action (see Ephesians 6:10–18).

What about those problematic Scripture passages in the Old Testament that suggest God is not always good? And what about Job? Scripture is quite clear that God allowed Satan to devastate Job. Sure, God restored Job in the end, but Job and his family were traumatized and tormented in the process.

Among the most basic principles for interpreting the Bible is allowing what is clear to interpret what is unclear. That is, when you come across a passage that appears strange and knotty, it's best to allow the parts of the Bible about which you are confident to govern how you think about the difficult portion. Don't let the confusing bits dominate your understanding. That doesn't mean don't wrestle with them, but don't let them dominate.

It's clear that Jesus is the most accurate representation of the Father, and that all of the Old Testament leads up to the life of Jesus (see John 5:19–20; Luke 24:27, 44). What this means, essentially, is that *the fact of Jesus's life, death, and resurrection requires that we reinterpret the Old Testament* (see 2 Corinthians 3:7–18). Many Jews in Jesus's day, not least the disciples, had to do this. Whatever first-century Jews might have thought the Law meant, it had to take on a new meaning in light of Jesus, who fulfilled the Law where Israel never could. Job is a fuzzy book, but the life of Jesus is clear. This makes Jesus a "higher" truth than Job. The gospel stories must dominate our thinking, rather than the Job story.

Simply put, *Jesus is the fullest representation of God's heart* (see John 14:7–9). In the New Testament, the apostle Paul declared the supremacy of Christ by describing Him as the image of the invisible God and the fullness of God (Colossians 1:15, 19). The life of Jesus is essentially the best witness to God's intentions for humankind. Jesus healed everyone He encountered (see Appendix III). This fact is compelling and must be given its proper weight as extraordinary evidence that the will of our Father in heaven is *for all to be healed*. "God's will isn't revealed in the afflictions Jesus encountered, but in His loving and powerful response to those afflictions."[12]

BALM OF LOVE

How could I ever have thought You
to be the cause of these wounds
for the longer I gaze at You
the more my aching sores
begin to heal
How is it that it's taken
me this long to see
Your love is the balm
my heart truly needs

by Jai Gaurangi

Appendix III

A. BIBLE VERSES ABOUT HEALING

Jesus went throughout Galilee, teaching in their synagogues, preaching the good news of the kingdom, and healing every disease and sickness among the people. News about him spread all over Syria, and people brought to him all who were ill with various diseases, those suffering severe pain, the demon-possessed, those having seizures, and the paralyzed; and he healed them. (Matthew 4:23–24)

Then Jesus said to the centurion, "Go! It will be done just as you believed it would." And his servant was healed at that moment. (Matthew 8:13)

When Jesus came into Peter's house, he saw Peter's mother-in-law lying in bed with a fever. He touched her hand and the fever left her, and she got up and began to wait on him. When evening came, many who were demon-possessed were brought to him, and he drove out the spirits with a word and healed all the sick. (Matthew 8:14–16)

Jesus turned and saw her. "Take heart, daughter," he said, "your faith has healed you." And the woman was healed at that moment. (Matthew 9:22)

Jesus went through all the towns and villages, teaching in their synagogues, proclaiming the good news of the kingdom and healing every disease and sickness. (Matthew 9:35)

But the Pharisees went out and plotted how they might kill Jesus. Aware of this, Jesus withdrew from that place. A large crowd followed him, and he healed all who were ill. He warned them not to tell others about him. (Matthew 12:14–16)

Then they brought him a demon-possessed man who was blind and mute, and Jesus healed him, so that he could both talk and see. (Matthew 12:22)

When Jesus heard what had happened, he withdrew by boat privately to a solitary place. Hearing of this, the crowds followed him on foot from the towns. When Jesus landed and saw a large crowd, he had compassion on them and healed their sick. (Matthew 14:13–14)

And when the men of that place recognized Jesus, they sent word to all the surrounding country. People brought all their sick to him and begged him to let the sick just touch the edge of his cloak, and all who touched it were healed. (Matthew 14:35–36)

Then Jesus said to her, "Woman, you have great faith! Your request is granted." And her daughter was healed at that moment. (Matthew 15:28)

Jesus rebuked the demon, and it came out of the boy, and he was healed at that moment. (Matthew 17:18)

The whole town gathered at the door, and Jesus healed many who had various diseases. He also drove out many demons, but he would not let the demons speak because they knew who he was. (Mark 1:33–34)

A few days later, when Jesus again entered Capernaum, the people heard that he had come home. They gathered in such large numbers that there was no room left, not even outside the door, and he preached the word to them. Some men came, bringing to him a paralyzed man, carried by four of them. Since they could not get him to Jesus because of the crowd, they made an opening in the roof above Jesus by digging through it and then lowered the mat the man was lying on. When Jesus saw their faith, he said to the paralyzed man, "Son, your sins are forgiven." (Mark 2:1–5)

He could not do any miracles there, except lay his hands on a few sick people and heal them. (Mark 6:5)

"What do you want me to do for you?" Jesus asked him. The blind man said, "Rabbi, I want to see." "Go," said Jesus, "your faith has healed you." Immediately he received his sight and followed Jesus along the road. (Mark 10:51–52)

At sunset, the people brought to Jesus all who had various kinds of sickness, and laying his hands on each one, he healed them. (Luke 4:40)

One day Jesus was teaching and the Pharisees and teachers of the law were sitting there. They had come from every village of Galilee and from Judea and Jerusalem. And the power of the Lord was with Jesus to heal the sick. Some men came carrying a paralyzed man on a mat and tried to take him into the house to lay him before Jesus. When they could not find a way to do this because of the crowd, they went up on the roof and lowered him on his mat through the tiles into the middle of the crowd, right in front of Jesus. When Jesus saw their faith, he said, "Friend, your sins are forgiven." (Luke 5:17–20)

Even while the boy was coming, the demon threw him to the ground in a convulsion. But Jesus rebuked the impure spirit, healed the boy and gave him back to his father. (Luke 9:42)

On a Sabbath Jesus was teaching in one of the synagogues, and a woman was there who had been crippled by a spirit for eighteen years. She was bent over and could not straighten up at all. When Jesus saw her, he called her forward and said to her, "Woman, you are set free from your infirmity." Then he put his hands on her, and immediately she straightened up and praised God. (Luke 13:10–13)

Now on his way to Jerusalem, Jesus traveled along the border between Samaria and Galilee. As he was going into a village, ten men who had leprosy met him. They stood at a distance and called out in a loud voice, "Jesus, Master, have pity on us!" When he saw them, he said, "Go, show yourselves to the priests." And as they went, they were cleansed. One of them, when he saw he was healed, came back, praising God in a loud voice. He threw himself at Jesus's feet and thanked him—and he was a Samaritan. Jesus asked, "Were not all ten cleansed? Where are the other nine? Has no one returned to give praise to God except this foreigner?" Then he said to him, "Rise and go; your faith has made you well." (Luke 17:11–19)

Jesus said to him, "Receive your sight; your faith has healed you." Immediately he received his sight and followed Jesus, praising God. When all the people saw it, they also praised God. (Luke 18:42–43)

And one of them struck the servant of the high priest, cutting off his right ear. But Jesus answered, "No more of this!" And he touched the man's ear and healed him. (Luke 22:50–51)

Once more he visited Cana in Galilee, where he had turned the water into wine. And there was a certain royal official whose son lay sick at Capernaum. When this man heard that Jesus had arrived in Galilee from Judea, he went to him and begged him to come and heal his son, who was close to death. "Unless you people see signs and wonders," Jesus told him, "you will never believe." The royal official said, "Sir, come down before my child dies." "Go," Jesus replied, "Your son will live." The man took Jesus at his word and departed. While he was still on the way, his servants met him with the news that his boy was living. (John 4:46–51)

Some time later, Jesus went up to Jerusalem for one of the festivals. Now there is in Jerusalem near the Sheep Gate a pool, which in Aramaic is called Bethesda and which is surrounded by five covered colonnades. Here a great number of disabled people used to lie—the blind, the lame, the paralyzed. One who was there had been an invalid for thirty-eight years. When Jesus saw him lying there and learned that he had been in this condition for a long time, he asked him, "Do you want to get well?" "Sir," the invalid replied, "I have no one to help me into the pool when the water is stirred. While I am trying to get in, someone else goes down ahead of me." Then Jesus said to him, "Get up! Pick up your mat and walk." At once the man was cured; he picked up his mat and walked. (John 5:1–9)

As he went along, he saw a man blind from birth. His disciples asked him, "Rabbi, who sinned, this man or his parents, that he was born blind?" "Neither this man nor his parents sinned," said Jesus, "but this happened so that the works of God might be displayed in him. As long as it is day, we must do the works of him who sent me. Night is coming, when no one can work. While I am in the world, I am the light of the world." After saying this, he spit on the ground, made some mud with the saliva, and put it on the man's eyes. "Go," he told him, "wash in the Pool of Siloam" (this word means "Sent"). So the man went and washed, and came home seeing. (John 9:1–7)

You know what has happened throughout the province of Judea, beginning in Galilee after the baptism that John preached—how God anointed Jesus of Nazareth with the Holy Spirit and power, and how he went around doing good and healing all who were under the power of the devil, because God was with him. (Acts 10:37–38)

B. BIBLE VERSES ABOUT MEDICINE

Some Christians believe the pursuit of medical treatment is contrary to faith in God's healing power. Yet the Bible contends that faith in God and acceptance of modern medicine are not mutually exclusive. To be sure, medicine is a manifestation of God's healing power. God is the creator of all things seen and unseen, including the human body and the medicine that heals it. God can heal supernaturally, and sometimes He does, but often He chooses to release His healing through human hands. Either way, God is the source of all healing.

The Bible describes numerous occasions when medical intervention preceded healing and therefore authorizes its use:

Isaiah said, "Prepare a poultice of figs and apply it to the boil, and he will recover." (Isaiah 38:21)

Is there no balm in Gilead? Is there no physician there? Why then is there no healing for the wound of my people? (Jeremiah 8:22)

"Babylon will suddenly fall and be broken. Wail over her! Get balm for her pain; perhaps she can be healed." (Jeremiah 51:8)

"Son of man, I have broken the arm of Pharaoh king of Egypt. It has not been bound up to be healed or put in a splint so that it may become strong enough to hold a sword." (Ezekiel 30:21)

"Fruit trees of all kinds will grow on both banks of the river. Their leaves will not wither, nor will their fruit fail. Every month they will bear fruit because the water from the sanctuary flows to them. Their fruit will serve for food and their leaves for healing." (Ezekiel 47:12)

Jesus answered them, "It is not the healthy who need a doctor, but the sick." (Luke 5:31)

Our dear friend Luke, the doctor, and Demas send greetings. (Colossians 4:14)

Stop drinking only water, and use a little wine because of your stomach and your frequent illnesses. (1 Timothy 5:23)

On hearing this, Jesus said, "It is not the healthy who need a doctor, but the sick." (Matthew 9:12)

But a Samaritan, as he traveled, came where the man was; and when he saw him, he took pity on him. He went to him and bandaged his wounds, pouring on oil and wine. Then he put the man on his own donkey, brought him to an inn and took care of him. (Luke 10:33–34)

Appendix IV

SPIRITUAL RISK FACTORS
FOR DISEASE

It is well documented in the literature that our mental-emotional health and spiritual health impact our physical health. While many diseases have an unknown cause, some have risk factors. A risk factor is something that increases a person's chance of developing a particular disease; for example, we know that obesity can contribute to type II diabetes, and high blood pressure is linked to heart disease. But we also know that not everyone who is obese or hypertensive has diabetes or heart disease and that often people develop a disease without having any obvious risk factors. It is important, therefore, to distinguish correlation from causation. A risk factor may be *correlated* with disease but is not necessarily the *cause* of that disease.

Risk factors can be either controllable or uncontrollable. For example, avoiding tobacco use reduces one's risk for lung cancer (controllable), while a genetic mutation in the BRCA1 or BRCA2 gene increases one's risk for breast cancer (uncontrollable).

Risk factors can also be mental-emotional and spiritual. In her book *Molecules of Emotion,* the late Dr. Candace Pert revealed, through her groundbreaking research, the biomolecular basis of emotions. Dr. Pert discovered that peptides, which are small protein fragments, are the substance of emotions. Her revolutionary work provides tangible evidence that our bodies and minds are an interconnected system, and our thoughts and emotions can impact our health.[13]

Stress is a good example of an emotional risk factor.[14] It increases the body's production of cortisol, a hormone that can produce memory loss and depression, and adrenaline, a hormone and neurotransmitter that impacts the blood vessels, heart, respiratory system, and immune system. To cope with stress, some people turn to harmful habits like smoking, alcohol abuse, and overeating. All can adversely affect health.

Spiritual risk factors are what the Bible calls "bitter roots" (Hebrews 12:15). Bitter roots have been identified by John and Paula Sandford (Elijah House Ministries) and Francis and Judith MacNutt (Christian Healing Ministries), who are highly respected pioneers in healing prayer ministry. Bitter roots include our judgments, expectancies, inner vows, and foundational lies, which are underpinned by bitterness, resentment, and unforgiveness.[15] Bitter roots create potential entry points for unwelcome spiritual forces to facilitate disease (see Ephesians 4:26–27, 31–32).

It's important for cancer fighters to aggressively attack their disease by eliminating all controllable risk factors (physical, mental-emotional, and spiritual) through lifestyle changes, medical treatment, counseling, and healing prayer.

Cancer is an extremely complex disease, and in most

cases, its cause is unknown. It originates, presumably, from some combination of controllable and uncontrollable factors. Our inclination as human beings is to speculate the cause of one's cancer, but it's important to walk humbly as Jesus did and avoid judgmental and naive conclusions that insinuate blame. To do so only increases emotional burden and is counterproductive to healing.

Afterword

"I have fought the good fight,
I have finished the race,
I have kept the faith."

2 Timothy 4:7

It has been healing to write my story here. There are pieces I have left out and pieces that have yet to be written. These pages are only a snapshot, a slice of my journey. Often when I re-read it, it feels surreal. *Did I really have cancer?* Yes there are embers out of the corner of my eye, but their remnants are softened by the beauty and wonder and majesty of life. I am watching my children grow into beautiful human beings.

Cancer has never been my identity, and I have never asked "why". Even the questions I once pondered are now crumpled among my mismatched socks. My spirit is on fire for my Lord and Savior Jesus Christ, and I am committed to living out of the freshness of each new day.

HANDS OF GOD

Despite the aching solitude,
the crippling fear
and the heartbreak,
there is also an unshakeable sense
of love, unity, prayer, and community
that rises from the embers of this age
until one day we find
all that would be remembered of this time
is that no matter how hard things got
our hearts remained safe
in the hands of God

by Jai Gaurangi

Acknowledgements

My heartfelt thanks and gratitude to each of you:

My loving and supportive family, especially my mom, Joanne Marker, who carried my heart in hers.

Toni-Ann Parenteau, the Lord knew that you were the one I needed in that critical moment. I will always remember your comfort, strength, and love.

My prayer ministers Linda Guite, Debbie McKinniss, Alecia Davidson, and Judy Davis. Thank you for walking with me and persevering through the hard work of intercession that brought me freedom.

Pastor Rick McKinniss, I can't imagine how this trip would have gone without you. Your wisdom, care, and affirmation of me and my ministry will always be treasured.

Mary Danahy, my friend and comrade. You brought joy and light to a time of sorrow and darkness.

Anne Abramson, Terri Mostoller, and Margie Rodgers, my Lancaster Way neighbors and super-support team. I don't know what my family would have done without you. Our little village has weathered many storms, but we are forever bound and strong.

Lay Kuan Toh, my comrade and prayer partner. You breathed life into my ministry and have been an encouragement to me since we met. I am grateful for your keen eye and insight that have made this a much better book.

Even though we live oceans apart, our hearts will always be connected.

Rosanne Magnoli and Barbara Schweitzer, my comrades, friends, and prayer partners. I am forever grateful for your love, encouragement, and feedback on this book. Your longstanding dedication to our prayer ministry is humbling and keeps my heart full.

Pastor Willard Baumgartner, your support, encouragement, and faithful partnership in ministry has been a great blessing to me and the kingdom of God.

Patricia Gigliotti, my beautiful friend and prayer partner. You are a force in my life and a force for Jesus. Your spiritual insight is off the charts. Thank you for lending it to me for this book.

Mandy Adendorff, my cherished friend and mentor. You walked with me, believed in me, and spoke life into my spirit and kingdom destiny. (www.mandyadendorff.com)

Bishop Arnold Muwonge, a brilliant and honorable man of God. You have changed my life profoundly. (www.destinyafrica.org)

Mike McKinniss, your teaching and encouragement have been a great help to me as I've wrestled with the hard stuff. Thank you for your contribution to this book.

Jai Gaurangi, thank you for allowing me to weave your beautiful words into the tapestry of my story. Your poetry is a gift to me and the world. (www.jaigaurangi.com)

Christy Distler of Avodah Editorial Services, your

excellent work and encouragement were a great boost to my manuscript. (www.avodaheditorialservices.com)

Thank you to the many other people who prayed for me, loved me, and encouraged me in all your beautifully unique ways.

Author Bio

Joellen Putnam began her career as an analytical chemist and scientific project manager, then left the world of science to become a full-time stay-at-home mom.

Joellen has served extensively in multiple international prayer ministries, has been a project coordinator for several initiatives to unify the body of Christ, and has been active with the Kampala Children's Centre in Uganda, since 2009.

In 2015, Joellen founded Activate the Cure, a ministry devoted to fighting cancer with prayer. Its mission is to partner with God in the arena of cancer by praying with cancer fighters and long-term survivors, and praying for researchers working to find new treatments and a cure.

In her spare time, she enjoys hiking, boating, kayaking, and fiber-arts weaving. She lives on the Connecticut shoreline with her husband, with whom she has two adult children. For more information about Joellen's book and ministry, visit her website at www.joellenputnam.com.

Endnotes

[1] Oswald Chambers, My Utmost For His Highest Updated Edition, (Grand Rapids, Michigan: Discovery House Publishers, 1992), June 3 reading.

[2] Catherine Marshall, Beyond Ourselves (New York: Avon Books, 1963), 97.

[3] David Manuel, Once Upon a Prayer: How to Hear God in Your Heart (Hagerstown, Maryland: McDougal Publishing Company, 2004).

[4] Dr. Irene Kraeger, *The Mindful Christian* (Minneapolis: Fortress Press, 2020).

[5] Lynn Eib, *When God and Cancer Meet* (Carol Stream, Illinois: Tyndale Momentum, 2002).

[6] Lynn Eib, *Peace in the Face of Cancer* (Carol Stream, Illinois: Tyndale Momentum, 2017).

[7] Abraham Kuyper, The Work of the Holy Spirit (New York: Cosimo Books, 2007).

[8] J. D. Greear, *Stop Asking Jesus into Your Heart: How to Know for Sure You Are Saved* (Nashville: B&H Books, 2013), 5.

[9] Ibid.

[10] Gregory A. Boyd, *Is God to Blame? Pat Answers to the Problem of Suffering* (Madison, Wisconsin: InterVar-

sity Press, 2003), 87.

[11] Gregory A. Boyd, "The Point of the Book of Job", ReKnew.org, October 16, 2018.

[12] Boyd, *Is God to Blame?*, 91.

[13] Candace B. Pert, Ph.D., *Molecules of Emotion: The Science Behind Mind-Body Medicine* (New York: Pocket Books, 1999).

[14] Sheldon Cohen, Denise Janicki-Deverts, William J. Doyle, Gregory E. Miller, Ellen Frank, Bruce S. Rabin, and Ronald B. Turner, "Chronic stress, glucocorticoid receptor resistance, inflammation, and disease risk," National Academy of Sciences, April 2, 2012, https://www.sciencedaily.com/releases/2012/04/120402162546.htm.

[15] John Loren and Paula Sandford, Transforming the Inner Man: God's Powerful Principles for Inner Healing and Lasting Life Change (Lake Mary, Florida: Charisma House, 2007).

Index

SOME WAYS GOD SPEAKS TO US

Bible, 89, 133
Creative ways, 180
Coincidences,145
Divine timing, 26
Encouraging words, 129
Friends, 76
Gift of medicine, 62
His creatures, 117
His presence, 98, 138
Holy Spirit, 54
Intimate encounters, 11
Lives of other people, 22
Name of Jesus, 47
Numbers in the Bible, 161
Our children, 40
Our doubt, 172
Our memories, 17
Our questions, 51
Our story, 157
Pastors and teachers, 36
Peace, 68, 123
Prayer, 168
Prayers and kindnesses of others, 150
Songs, 93
Scripture directly into our spirit, 81
Spirit of thankfulness, 30
Symbols, 187
Voice of the Holy Spirit, 105
Wisdom of others, 72
With authority, 112

The light shines in the darkness, and
the darkness has not overcome it.

John 1:5

Heart Notes

Heart Notes

Heart Notes

Heart Notes

Heart Notes

Heart Notes

Heart Notes

Heart Notes

Heart Notes

Heart Notes

Made in United States
Troutdale, OR
01/27/2024

17194420R00148